Retriever Pups

The Formative First Year

Bill Tarrant

Voyageur Press

The excerpts from *The Covenant of the Wild: Why Animals Chose Domestication* that appear on page 26 are reprinted by permission of Stephen Budiansky. Copyright ©1992 by Stephen Budiansky.

Excerpts from *Snakefoot: The Making of a Champion* appear throughout by permission of Bob Wehle. Copyright © 1996 by Robert G. Wehle.

Edited by Todd R. Berger
Designed by Kristy Tucker
Printed in Hong Kong

99   00   01   02   03   5   4   3   2   1

Library of Congress Cataloging-in-Publication Data

Tarrant, Bill.
   Retriever pups : the formative first year / Bill Tarrant.
       p.   cm.—(Master training series)
   Includes index.
   ISBN 0-89658-383-X
   1. Retrievers—Training. 2. Hunting dogs—Training. I. Title.
   II. Series.
   SF429.R4T377   1999
   636.752'735—dc21   98-45205
                                             CIP

Distributed in Canada by Raincoast Books,
8680 Cambie Street, Vancouver, B.C. V6P 6M9

Published by Voyageur Press, Inc.
123 North Second Street, P.O. Box 338, Stillwater, MN 55082 U.S.A.
651-430-2210, fax 651-430-2211

Educators, fundraisers, premium and gift buyers, publicists, and marketing managers:
Looking for creative products and new sales ideas? Voyageur Press books are available at special discounts when purchased in quantities, and special editions can be created to your specifications. For details contact the marketing department at 800-888-9653.

Page 1: *An eight-week old yellow Lab pup. (Photograph © William H. Mullins)*

A Chesapeake Bay retriever puppy. (Photograph © Kent and Donna Dannen)

Above: *An adult golden on a glorious summer day. (Photograph © Bill Buckley/The Green Agency)*
Page 6: *Waiting for ducks in a Montana marsh. (Photograph © Bill Buckley/The Green Agency)*

Acknowledgments

The author extends special gratitude to Larry Anderson, Jim Culbertson, Butch Goodwin, Barbara Newsome, and Jim Ruppel for providing some of the superb photographs for this book. Also, the author is deeply indebted to the late Clarence J. Pfaffenberger, for the report of his (and the late Peter Scott's) dog research, in *The New Knowledge of Dog Behavior*.

Dedication

For Boyd Hamilton
Luke 10:25–37

Also by Bill Tarrant

Best Way to Train Your Gun Dog

Hey Pup, Fetch It Up

Bill Tarrant's Gun Dog Book: A Treasury of Happy Tails

Problem Gun Dogs

Tarrant Trains Gun Dogs: A Treasury of Happy Tails

Training the Hunting Retriever: The New Approach

How To Hunt Birds with Gun Dogs

Pick of the Litter

Training the Versatile Retriever to Hunt Upland Game

The Magic of Dogs

Gun Dog Training: New Strategies from Today's Top Trainers

The Field & Stream Upland Bird Hunting Handbook

Table of Contents

Prologue

The wind-chopped lake flickers like hammered copper in dawn's light. Brittle stems left over from summer's weeds snap, broken-backed, with the hunter's step. Tilted sideways by the weight of the decoy sack, the man stops at water's edge while the Lab and he read the lake, the wind, and the wan, eastern light.

"Whataya think?" he asks the dog.

The Lab's long, black body presses into the man's waders, the dog glancing up with happy eyes as his tail beats on the man's calf. "Let's go over there," the man tells him.

Hush-breathing as he walks—something he picked up years ago, always hunting alone—the man soon says to the dog, "You gonna get a bird?"

The Lab leaps to slam through the tules, the man yelling after him, "Think so, huh?"

Suddenly the retriever stops and serpentines the length of his body before the man—like the wave that fans make at a football game. He is that excited, that happy.

The man chuckles, then says no more. So the sounds that are left are the wind, the creaking tree limbs, the chi-chi birds fluttering in the branches, the soft slosh of shore water on the man's waders, and the call of a hawk far, far away.

That's what this book's about: *sensing the whole of nature.* Bringing the dog to master craftsmanship by hunting, not by training. Being the dog's helpmate and his buddy, not his trainer, and mighty seldom his disciplinarian.

This book is about learning what a retriever is and what nature is. A Chesie like this has a lot to tell you. (Photograph © Lon E. Lauber)

That retriever pup you've adopted will take you to a better world. And if you can't see that world, nor understand that world, nor appreciate that world, nor want that world, then I really wonder why you'd want the dog. Because what I've described above is his (or her) world: the out-of-doors.

That dog is your ticket to nature: your guide, your mentor, your sixth sense, your one true buddy who never tells the guys back home you fell face-down in the marsh.

The point is this: If you can't read the retriever's world, then you're traveling in a foreign land when you hunt.

Just this weekend I was again saddened by retriever field trial people. They were having fun with their retrievers running marks and blinds—and it is fun—but continually field trialers make it more and more rigid, mechanical, contrived, and unnatural.

At no time did I find one handler reading the dog or reading the land. Can you imagine that? Why else be out there? At first glance you, the handler, must be able to decipher what confronts your dog—the gully, the hill, the copse of woods, the lake, the wind, the light, the odors—and know what each of them means to Pup. For that's his world. That's where he works. And you must know what it all means. For if you don't know a thing about the backcountry outside your city limits, you're sure penalizing Pup's performance by being a dumb teacher.

Plus, you must be able to read your dog—his eyes, the tilt of his head, the angulation of his rear legs, his trembling, his cocked ears. For example, what does it mean when Pup leaps on your back?

You must know what your dog's telling you with but a glance. For if you don't, you can't help him do what you want him to do. You should know him like your tongue knows the back of your teeth. You should be able to read his (or her) mood and intent every second in the field.

I have little hope for so many any more. It's gotten to the point where I expect to find tomorrow's field trial retriever trainer—in this world of glamour-tech—incorporating a surveyor's tripod, a sextant, and a compass. Maybe one day a satellite service will transmit a picture of the running retriever on a computer screen. The entire bird hunt will be conducted in a domed stadium with rubber-lined ponds, plastic foliage, and fiberglass rocks. And the handler won't recognize the difference.

What's the matter with us? I know the city's robbed so many of us of what's necessary, beautiful, vital, and mending. If the anti-gun zealots, primarily city people, lived with the land, they would have sons and daughters who were marksmen, a deer would hang in their woodshed. And fathers would feel as equal to their surroundings in the woods as they do today on a tennis court. And the anti-hunters would know how a 7½ shell patterned, instead of how broccoli sprouts should be brought to the table.

Do you know only 4 percent of Americans live on a farm today? No wonder we've lost all love and knowledge of the land. Lost as well is the make-do to prime a well, pull a calf, doctor an udder, shoe a horse, sharpen a scythe.

We are a puny and helpless lot. God help us. And helping us is exactly what God does each time you adopt a retriever pup. He gives you a first-class ticket to the wilderness and the best buddy on earth to go there with. He gives you back your roots, your resourcefulness, and your vitality. That is if you are a hunter. If you are a field trialer, then forget it.

I honestly saw one field trial handler—a well-meaning person who truly loves his dog and deserves better—with his Lab running for a distant blind (that's a planted bird the dog has not seen fall). The man held up his right hand (palm facing away) and extended his index finger and his little finger to make something like football goal posts, and he looked in that space over the back of his hand and said to all of us, "This is what the field trial judges are doing now. If that dog strays outside this frame of two fingers, he's out of contention."

My Sweet Father Who Is In Heaven, what on earth is wrong with us? Do those two extended fingers have knowledge of the slope of the land, the way the wind's blowing, the goat heads in the field, the hot spots of last-night's scent that Pup is encountering?

What if Pup's in a rape field on a hot day? If he is, he couldn't smell a hog lot fifty feet from him, and those goal-post fingers wouldn't be telling the handler a damned thing.

Why hold up fingers and go through all this and other mechanical and electronic tomfoolery when it's you that's deficient? Never the dog. You. Because you don't know the first thing about the natural world you want to excel in.

Plus, you won't let the dog be a living creature. If you're the average field trialer or test hunt participant, you make of him a robot, a chess pawn. You make a bionic dog.

A hunting retriever doesn't run to look good on some judge's score sheet. He runs to get you a bird. The dog trained and handled in a field trial performs for man's vanity. And man's vanity is the dog's doom. But the Pup you train to hunt runs to get you a bird and gives you a golden day afield.

Why do so many forget this?

Well, that's what this book's about. Learning what a retriever is and what nature is. Learning that retrievers always cast the way their head is pointing. Learning that swimming retrievers do not want to turn into the wind. Then learning, as well, how to put the land and water and wind and dog together to get birds.

If that's what you want, then read on. If not, then I apologize, for I can't help you. This book just isn't into making mechanical dogs in an unnatural world.

Instead, this book is for the guy or gal who realizes both they and their retrievers are God's creatures, that the retriever excels in the wild, that getting a bird is their mutual goal. So to help the dog, the man must learn all he can about the wild. And having done this, for the man and dog to proceed sensibly together as bonded hunters in the bird field. And by hunting, the dog is trained. Not the other way around.

It don't get no better than this. And nowhere does it make more sense.

This is Jessie, a hunting retriever, who epitomizes all we hope to accomplish in this book. Here she finds, flushes, and fetches a prairie chicken in the Flinthills of Kansas. (Photograph © Larry Anderson and Jim Culbertson)

The Wolf that Came in from the Wild

"Outside a dog a book is man's best friend. Inside a dog it's too dark to read."
—Groucho Marx

You're right, Groucho, but now's one time we've got to get both inside the book and inside the dog. What is he? How did he come to be? What makes him tick? How's the best way to raise and train him? In other words, just what is a dog?

Well, to understand that, we must first understand neoteny. Pronounced knee-ought-toe-knee, this concept is simple, so don't run away.

Neoteny is a powerful tool for the humane trainer who wants dogs trained without fingerprints. Neoteny is an insight into the core nature of the dog. Knowing neoteny will help you understand Pup better and therefore train and work and live with him with greater understanding.

If it weren't for the reality of neoteny, it is doubtful if humans would ever have had a dog. And wouldn't that be a downer?

WHAT NEOTENY MEANS

For our purposes, neoteny is defined as a wolf that never matures. Thus the eternal puppy becomes the domesticated dog, primarily because he can transfer his pack instinct and submissiveness to the human partner, who he accepts as the Alpha, or dominant, male.

The wolf is the hunting Lab's ancestor. The dog threw itself in with man primarily because of its pack instinct and its desire to submit. (Photograph © Gary Kramer)

Physical Characteristics of Neoteny

Signs of neoteny in a domesticated dog are, in part, doming of the skull, shortening of the muzzle, hanging ears, short hair, and an upright tail. These are physical characteristics found in the wolf puppy but outgrown by adulthood, yet in a domesticated dog these characteristics may be evident throughout the dog's life, depending on selective breeding.

Another aspect of neoteny is that the domestic dog remains dependent on the substitute Alpha male, which is the human partner. But the wolf, seeking independence and considering his own self the Alpha male, bolts to the wild for he bears no allegiance and has no sense of obedience to anyone. The domestic dog maintains perpetual youthfulness as evidenced by his submission.

Mutation

Now these physical and psychological changes that occurred in dogs and resulted in human adoption are not mutations. *Webster's New World Dictionary* tells us, "a mutation is a sudden variation in some inheritable characteristic in a germ cell of an individual animal or plant, as distinguished from a variation resulting from generations of gradual change."

Those variations resulting from generations of gradual change describe the concept of neoteny. The neotenization of the wolf that produced the dog with characteristics ideal for domestication were—as discovered by scientists in various fields—caused by the wolves' need to adapt to successive comings and goings of ice-age glaciers. And it is interesting to note, these glaciers lasted millions of years and ended only 10,000 years ago, which is the general date researchers find that dog and man united.

But know this. The evidence of man and wolf intermittently or loosely associating dates back thousands of years, before domestication became a reality. There never was some ancient contract where on a given day man said, "You move in with me and guard my place and help me hunt, and I'll feed you and keep you warm and protect you from your enemies."

Hardly. The folk story of a caveman's child finding a wolf pup and toting it home, pleading "Daddy can I keep it?" was not the case.

Domestication

Humans have an uneven record as domesticators. Native Americans kept moose, raccoon, bears, baby buffalo, and bald eagles as pets, but none

The domestic dog generally has a shortened nose, floppy ears, a domed head, and short hair, plus an upright tail. (Photograph © Gary Kramer)

were domesticated. Ancient Egyptians tried to domesticate gazelles, ibex, hyenas, and antelope but failed. On the other hand, humans were successful in domesticating some animals, such as sheep, goats, horses, and cows.

So why could some animals be domesticated while others remained wild? It's a matter of biology, or neoteny, since all domesticated animals exhibit perpetual immaturity. For an animal to lend itself to domesticity, it has to possess specific traits. These are:

1) A high reproduction rate to produce in excess of what any human population could accommodate, thus guaranteeing a perpetual supply.

2) Lack of fear to maintain the ability to confront new realities and not crack up or bolt.

3) Submissiveness, so the animal does not bite the hand that feeds it nor insist on its own way but accommodates man by saying, "Okay, if

that's the way you want it."

The Wolf Comes in from the Wild

The domesticated dog chose man as much as man chose the dog. The tableau unfolds: Man and wolf/dog intermingling for centuries, all the while neoteny continues to produce a different kind of wolf, and when those changes result in the traits listed above, domestication becomes possible.

Consider, even today the wolf is known as a northern dweller. So it can be assumed the wolf stayed in the cold of the ice age. But the neotenized wolf that became the domestic dog apparently chose the southern extremity of these ice movements.

Therefore, is it possible he developed the foreshortened nose since he lived in a warm climate? Yet the wolf, who stayed to the north, needed a long muzzle to filter the frigid air. Note: The wolf's muzzle and orbits compose nearly half of its whole head.

And is this why the wolf's coat remained long, but the neotenized dog's coat (sometimes) grew short?

Who knows? I make but guesses. Yet you deserve more than guesses, so I grabbed my duffel and headed for Kansas State University to visit with James Roush, a whiz-bang D.V.M. specializing in orthopedics.

Dr. James Roush

I laid our quest before him. "Why would the cold shorten a dog's muzzle?"

"Hum," he hushed softly, as is his way. "Neotenization occurred over millions of years. The same forces that are supposed to have created Asian and Native American features, that is smaller features, were likely the cold and all that went with it.

"To more readily escape frostbite man developed smaller facial features. Smaller ears to evade freezing, a smaller nose, which is exactly what happened to the dog.

"Now the warm-climate individual, such as the African, had to handle humidity and heat so evolution developed features such as a large nose and more sweat glands. Evolution always gives a creature the best adaptive features to handle his environment's requirements."

I enjoyed the afternoon with this bright, young scholar, and the explanation we came to get, we got. The cold was indeed responsible for neotenization of the wolf, which produced our precious dogs.

This many-time-great-great granddaughter of the wolf fetches a cinnamon teal for her human partner.

Selective breeding has transformed the domestic dog to stretch from the Irish wolfhound to the Chihuahua. This golden pup lies somewhere in the middle. (Photograph © William H. Mullins)

But don't charge me saying, "That don't hold water. A Labrador retriever is built like a wolf, but he has a short coat. How could that be?"

Simple—selective breeding. Man has so transformed the domestic dog as to stretch it from the Irish wolfhound, which weighs more than 110 pounds, to the Chihuahua, which is minuscule at two and one-quarter pounds.

I ask you to consider the Pomeranian. Once a shepherd named after a region of Prussia, this dog came to the eye of Queen Victoria while she was visiting Florence in 1888. The queen's preference for lap dogs prompted the selective breeding that saw these dogs mightily "shrunk."

TRAINABILITY AND NATURAL ABILITY

The domesticated dog brings with him two wolf instincts: the desire 1) to hunt and 2) to function as part of a pack. The hunting instinct in the retriever, for example, harvests the man a bird. The packing instinct drives the retriever to submit to his human partner as part of his sense of hierarchy; he gives the man the bird.

The Austrian Nobel Prize winner Konrad Z. Lorenz writes in his book *Man Meets Dog*, "The [wolf] does not possess those Oedipus complexes of the more domesticated dog which converts his master to a cross between a father and a god."

The dog regards and reveres a human as combination father and god, but the wolf would scoff and say, "Him? He's no big deal." So are you beginning to understand why I remain perpetually livid with a man (or woman) who would violently and unconscionably torture an adoring dog to compliance?

INHUMANITY BY OMISSION

And let's get this torture, inhumanity, or negligence straight. I don't just mean beating. What about malnutrition? What about filthy housing? What about working the dog until it collapses? Yes, there are all types of inhumanity.

Is there not inhumanity in denying a dog medical care? Right now my wife and I have a dog suffering from a fatal disease. The present treatment is difficult to adjust as needed and has many "sickly" side affects. So I set out to exhaust all alternatives, not to prolong the dog's life but to make what life she had left comfortable. And by perseverance, I discovered a brand new, approved medicine that saw 95 percent of dogs in a test study suffering no side affects. The medicine has proven effective. My own vet had never heard of the medicine, so I presented the literature to her.

For me to have accepted the status quo would have been inhumane, just like denying a dog exercise, proper nutrition, or human companionship.

Man gets away with mistreatment because all the dog desires is to do whatever the human partner wants. Each of us deals with a grown pup; it is never a lesser wolf the man mistreats. No matter the age of the domesticated dog, it is forever a pup. And it breaks my heart to think anyone would hurt or deny one of these innocent and compulsively loving creatures.

ANOTHER PERSPECTIVE

Now there is this. In his brilliant book *The Farmer's Dog*, British sheep herder John Holmes tells us, "The dog is not almost human, but man can easily become almost canine and take on the role of pack leader."

Let this distinction remain in the mind of the American retriever

A dog must be trainable but have natural ability. (Photograph © Gary Kramer)

trainer. It is the man's (or the woman's) obligation to mimic the dog, not demand the dog become human. To this end I love a quote from Corey Ford, the legendary *Field & Stream* humorist. Corey wrote, "Properly trained, a man can be dog's best friend."

Thanks, Corey, for it us, the humans, who should be the ones doing the thinking, the experimenting, offering the prospect of bonding. It is us who must initiate—and imitate. It is us who must be trained.

Training as Momma-Dog Does

How many times have I visited with you in column and book about emulating Momma-dog in training pups? She leaps forward with mock malice, her eyes but slits, her jowls slack and teeth glistening, her hot breath of opprobrium blasting the kid in the face. But it is all a toothless fight, just an act. Yet the pup does as she bids.

Man as a dog teacher is most effective when he takes on a similar role. So let man be the role model for the pup, especially because this isn't some dog we're trying to bring along. It's a perpetual puppy, whose inclination is to play and have but momentary concentration, and wants you to love him (or her) rather than make all those verbal noises and throw your arms around.

By recognizing Pup for what he is—a dog that never grew up—it is then possible for you to approach him as a child and not as a reasoning adult. Yet too many of us issue a command, and if it is not obeyed, we are quick to threaten or even inflict pain.

I don't think we'd be so inclined if we continually thought of Pup as a pup. Especially when it is realized that since Pup joined man (10,000 to 15,000 years ago, depending upon your authority) he has been selectively bred. And as the world's top dog breeder, Bob Wehle of Elhew Kennels in Alabama and New York has told me, "You select for breeding those dogs that please you."

Biddable and Submissive

And what is a pleasing dog? One that is biddable and easily trained, submissive and loyal to the Alpha male—you.

So not only do you have perpetual puppyhood in the domesticated dog due to neoteny, but you've also got thousands of years of selective breeding to make the domestic dog compliant and desirous of pleasing. All of which should make training a dog a pretty easy undertaking, wouldn't you say?

But there is this problem.

What is man selectively breeding for? There are two very important factors regarding the hunter and the selection of his dog. A dog must be trainable, yet have natural ability.

Now it is possible to hunt with a dog who proceeds only with natural ability. I know of many advanced retriever trainers (those who have moved to a higher plane) who are doing just this. They instill basic obedience so the dog will come back and not bolt for Alaska—then let him go. Let him bust brush, sweep across prairies, climb mountains, become as it is, a wild Indian.

Mike Gould of Kamiah, Idaho, is a master at this. The result is Mike's dog Camas, who at eight months old was leading high-priced clients on upland game hunts and not only getting the job done but also earning hefty tips for the handler.

Another illustration is the waterfowl guide who recently wrote and told me his dog had fetched more than three hundred client ducks before it was nine months old. And why just three hundred? The season came to an end!

Those two performances were made possible by natural ability.

The Dominant Trainer

But there are the dominant trainers and handlers who don't want to hazard the vicissitude of a dog striking out pell-mell, self-hunting, and casting where it feels could be points of opportunity. Why, such a dog might produce a rabbit, a bull snake, or a skunk.

It is the cautious and rigid owner, then, who demands trainability in his dog. This is the exact trainer who too often becomes brutal.

And I want to tell you something about this dominant trainer. Mike Gould insists, "Man wants to intimidate that which intimidates him." In other words, the dominant trainer wants absolute control of the dog to insure nothing goes wrong. Such a man is uncertain, unprepared for the rare event, and unwilling to take fate as it comes. Interesting, isn't it?

Is that the reason we have brutality in dog training? The trainer is afraid of that which he wants to control?

Approaching the End

Well, let's close this up by taking a final look at neoteny.

Pup should always be trained as a pup, as a child. (Photograph © Gary Kramer)

In one of the most important books of our time, *The Covenant of the Wild: Why Animals Chose Domestication,* Maryland-based writer Stephen Budiansky tells us, "There is one source of variation within a species that can be tapped—the change that all mammals and birds undergo in the course of developing from an infant to an adult. The range of variation that one sees within any adult population is minuscule compared with the differences that separate the average adult from the average juvenile. Both physical characteristics—everything from body shape and color to internal organs—and behavior change dramatically during development."

Budiansky continues, "if adulthood is reached before the 'normal' process of development is complete, some of the very striking youthful characteristics of the species will be locked in, while characteristically adult behaviors and structures are never developed or activated. Because the entire process of development is under genetic control, relatively small changes in the genes that determine the rate of development can produce enormous changes in the adult form . . .

"Neoteny is a way to introduce a whole slew of new traits very rapidly. It provides an abundance of raw material for specific new traits that might be an advantage in a new environment; it is a way to overcome the inherent limits that natural selection itself imposes on the variation that is available within any species, in any one generation, for natural selection to act upon."

Budiansky then observes the youth of any species "shows a curiosity about their surroundings, an ability to learn new things, a lack of fear of new situations, and even a nondiscriminating willingness to associate and play with members of other species . . ."

So the boldness and plasticity and curiosity—which is the key to intelligence—and the ability to learn new things could well be the definition of a puppy, right?

So when our domesticated dog is defined this way, does it not tell us how to train him? Or at least suggest how he should not be trained? Certainly it does. The dog must always be trained as a pup, as a child. And pain is not the way to do it.

You who deliver your child to a day-care center: is pain the way the caretakers achieve compliance? I hardly think so, but many trainers, especially the pros, feel it's all right to do so with a dog that is forever in adolescence.

But I can see what I'm up against; I ask the world to be kind and patient with their dog, while there are parents who kill their own children. Such realities are reported as child abuse in the courts. Autopsies show a child with a broken skull, another has been strangled, another burned, another beaten, and on and on.

You see the same story on TV and the parents so often look just like the couple next door or your own relatives. But there is a madness among us, and the result is torture and death for the helpless.

The dog fits the category of the defenseless. So please be kind in bringing your dog along.

And referring back to Groucho, who started off this chapter, I hope now inside your dog it's not too dark too read.

And so this book is begun.

(2)

Oh the Glory of a
New Pup

"Anyone who says you can't buy happiness, never bought a pup."
—Gene Hill, *Field & Stream*

Let's go get you a retriever pup. And let's do it right. No shopping mall pet shop, no backyard make-do. We want a pup from proven gun dog stock: parents that hunt many days every season and whose human companions keep them tuned up by Happy Timing them afield during the off-season.

What we really want is what Bob Wehle describes as a pup born *congenitally trained.* That's right. We want both the *natural ability* and the *trainability* in the dog.

NATURAL ABILITY

Well, natural ability, in part, is a full-bore nose, a power-driven set of wheels, and a great heart girth, so the rib cage can expand when Pup's running hard and he won't have to shut down. We also want intelligence and intensity. Get the idea? We want the best that good breeding and a gracious God can put in. We're not in the market for some factory-outlet wannabe.

TRAINABILITY

And trainability? That's a dog that's biddable, who wants to please, who is submissive, not always trying to take the power from you and run the

---

You want a pup from proven gun dog stock, from parents that hunt many days afield every season. (Photograph © Mark Kayser)

show. You've met that type. Yet this pliable dog is not a pushover; he's intelligent (and usually intense) and has learned what's fun and what value he has if he keeps you good company. This is a birdy dog who wants to please, won't quit, and has a lot of run in him for great field expanses, yet knowledge of the gun where he'll shut down and hunt close in heavy cover.

So that's natural ability and trainability, and we want both.

WHO TO TALK TO

Therefore what we do is this. We search out every 100-day-a-year bird hunter we've ever heard about. We ask him what dogs are getting the job done and where you can find them. NOW THIS WARNING! We are not looking for any field trial or test hunt hopefuls. The ribbon and trophy people have their own games and those games have little to do with a day's hunt afield.

Another place we ask around is the local gun dog club(s). Matter not the breed. Just ask them if they know who has a good hunting retriever. Bona fide dog people live dogs. They know dogs. They love dogs. They know who's who and who ain't. They'll direct you.

Just keep inquiring and eventually you're going to be standing on the doorstep of a bird hunter who knows his dog business. Ask to see his dogs work; he'll be proud to show you. Then ask if he has pups. If not, when will he have them? What will they cost? Can you get a guarantee on general health and genetic defects?

HEALTH

I'd say there's been a lot of negligent breeding since the time Labs and flat-coats originated from the same litters in Great Britain. Check flat-coat's bill of health below. The Lab list indicates what so often happens with popular breeds. Though it is the same dog—the only difference being length of coat—the flat-coat has a minimum number of defects compared to the Labrador. But in essence, they are twins.

The evidence is stark and graphic. The Lab has been popular, so inept breeders, wanting to make a buck, bred improperly and turned out genetically deficient animals. Whereas the flat-coat was never a popular dog, and only the devoted breeder reproduced them. The result is much fewer genetic deficiencies in the flat-coat breed than in the Labrador breed.

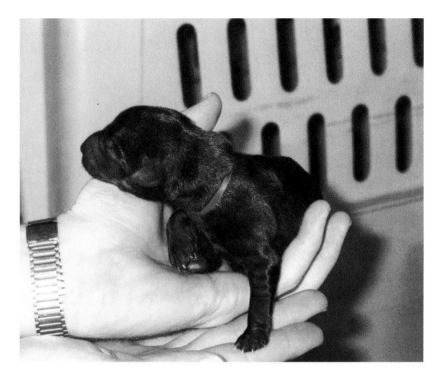

A one-day-old Lab pup. (Photograph © Barbara Newsome)

Congenital Diseases of Labrador and Flat-coat Retrievers

Labs: receptor dystrophy, bilateral cataracts, retinal dysplasia, central progressive retinal atrophy, postnatal cerebellar cortical degeneration, copper toxicosis, hemophilia A, congenital factor IX deficiency, bilateral carpal subluxation, craniomandibular osteopathy, hip dysplasia, muscular dystrophy, and hereditary myopathy, *plus twenty-one other identifiable congenital diseases.*

Flat-coat retrievers: hip dysplasia (low incidence), patellar luxation, histiosarcoma, glaucoma, epilepsy, diabetes insipidus, and megaesophagus.

For other retriever breeds and further information consult *Medical & Genetic Aspects of Purebred Dogs*, edited by Ross D. Clark, D.V.M., and Joan R. Stainer.

Ask the breeder if you can buy the pup on the basis of a vet's examination

You'd take a pup out of this sire: Insist on high-performance dogs. (Photograph © Lon E. Lauber)

and clearance. Serious breeders will appreciate feedback from veterinarians; they want to know how healthy their pups are.

But before getting so technical and clinical, you, yourself, can tell a lot just looking at the surroundings and the pups.

Is the place dirty? Does it stink? Are the other dogs well maintained? Are there feces left unattended? Is there plenty of fresh water? Could the houses use a coat of paint?

Anyone got a snotty nose, pus in the eyes, a messy rear end, an umbilical hernia? What about an undershot or overshot jaw? Drooling at the mouth, a discharge from the penis, skin eruptions on the belly, a pot belly that could indicate worms?

Look close—you're brighter than you think.

Are You a Hunter?

And while you're asking the breeder questions let's hope he is asking you a few of his own, such as, how many days a season do you hunt? The point being, many conscientious breeders won't sell a gun dog to a non-hunter or a once-upon-a-some-day hunter. They know what makes their dogs happy, and they want them into constant birds.

They also want their dogs in the house, watching TV, sleeping in your bedroom, and going everywhere in your pickup truck—especially to the fields where several times a week during the off-season you'll Happy Time Pup into birds. To isolate a dog in the backyard just won't do for these breeders; they want the best for Pup.

Don't Ever Malign the Vagabond

Know this. There are all types of people. You can find some of the best hunting retrievers in a hovel with bed springs in the ditch, a toilet stool in the driveway, and two families using the same outhouse. Proceed cautiously, but go ahead and look. You will be able to see and smell and "feel" the status of the place. The veterinarian can detect problems not evident to the puppy buyer's eyes, nose, and intuition.

And then, too, you'll find retrievers on suburban estates. Proceed cautiously here, as well. Too many people feel the rich can do everything right. I've met as many rich nuts as poor nuts. The rich can be superfluous. They may have so many leisure activities, the dogs have to be sandwiched between follies. Then again, there are men of means such as Bob Wehle, the English pointer specialist, who's lived his life as a dog philanthropist, and from him you'll get that one pup in a million.

I wrote in *Training the Versatile Retriever to Hunt Upland Game* that probably the best guy to buy a pup from is one who's on welfare and hunts every day. Except for being a good shot or receiving food stamps, this guy doesn't eat. He's a full-time hunter who probably has the best gun dog retriever you'll ever find.

I've lived with these guys. A loaf of bread, a slab of hoop cheese, some bologna, a tin of snuff—they wouldn't trade it all for a Balmoral-Castle-rolling-hills-hunt with accompanying banquet and a nod from the Queen. Don't ever ignore the frayed-cuff guy who's out at the elbows. I've learned more from them than all the others put together.

The moral of the story: Don't judge a book by its cover.

How Much Should a Pup Cost?

Engrave this in marble! The price you pay for a pup is irrelevant. How's that? Simple! In all you do, you have to do your own homework and make your own decisions. Price can be a factor in making a decision, but when buying a retriever, price paid is not necessarily proportional to hunting success. For a dog to cost thousands says nothing about his ability or his genetic predisposition to hunt. That's all we're looking for: HUNTING ABILITY! Don't get distracted and consider anything else. So the King of Siam owned the stud. What birds did he hunt in Siam? Get me? We want a hunting dog with a lot of bottom in him; we don't want no floss, no glitter, no press clippings.

Boy or Girl?

I don't know and I don't care what sex pup you have, but girls are usually more mellow, loving, insightful, and desirous of pleasing.

Boys are typically tagged as aggressive and competitive with the human companion—they want to be the Alpha male. They're also more reckless afield—they'll throw themselves into a thorn thicket—and they usually possess greater strength and endurance than the distaff.

Well, that's the usual. But it ain't like the King of Siam said, "So it is written, so it shall be." You can have female Labs who think they're bulldozers, whose boldness and birdiness is near lunatic. I remember Nodrog Penny, Gordon Olinger's brilliant little black bitch out in the Rockies. I competed with her one freezing day in the '60s, where the final field trial test was up and over a spiked and ice-glossed beaver dam. Penny conquered the dam then leaped back into the station wagon to suckle her litter of pups.

Then, too, there have been exceptional males. Mike Gould had the immortal Web, whose intensity and energy were so unmatched that when there was nothing to do he would scoop algae from the surface of farm ponds—just to be doing something. He gathered that green gunk, went ashore, spit it out, then launched to gather more. I'll be damned if some of his offspring don't do the same thing.

The point I make here is this: I hope you have one of these barnstormers. For you can take the spirit out of a dog—if you're mindless—but there's no way can you put it back in. Consequently, I don't spend my time picking a pup from a litter, I spend my time *praying*. There are only so many Michael-Jordan retrievers or Tiger-Woods retrievers sent down, and I hope to intercept one.

OTHER FACTORS

What color should the pup be? Big or small? Short or tall? On color I can tell you nearly all Labrador field trial champions are black—but why refer to field trials when we've just damned them? The only thing you really need to think about in body configuration is kinetic balance. What? Well, let's turn to that.

Now we're going to meet Mike Gould, the backwoods wizard of high-country Idaho, who I mentioned a little earlier. Mike's got different eyes than the rest of us. He sees things we never notice. That's because he's all dog and outback. There is nothing else in his world.

Mike used to live in Carbondale, Colorado. I'd visit him every summer and we'd train dogs, and fish the Roaring Fork River, and charcoal fajitas, and talk, and dream. We'd also go up 10,000 feet and run the Labs on blue grouse, and by fall, Mike's dogs were bona fide bird dogs. Nothing like blue grouse to put a feather edge on a dog.

RETRIEVER PUP FUNCTIONAL CONFORMATION

It was the inimitable Delmar Smith of Edmond, Oklahoma, the man who made the Brittany a bird dog in America, who first spoke to me of functional conformation. Delmar's a sure 'nuf idea man.

For our purposes, functional conformation is the shape of a dog that permits the animal to perform a function. The retrieving dog's function is to hunt and fetch game birds. For retrievers, an example of good

Louie, an absolutely beautiful eight-week-old Chesie pup. Note his stout forelegs, thick neck, blocky head. This pup will handle water. (Photograph © Butch Goodwin)

functional conformation would be a great heart girth (or rib cage), one larger than usual for the breed, so when the heart expands during hard work, the rib cage accommodates the greater size and therefore lets the dog keep hunting. If the rib cage were too small, the dog would have to shut down, for the heart could not expand and handle the dog's needs.

KINETIC BALANCE

Mike Gould read my description of functional conformation in *Best Way to Train Your Gun Dog*, and he ran with it, finally coming up with the breakthrough he calls kinetic balance.

Static balance: Balance while staying put.

Kinetic balance: Balance in motion.

Read on.

BODY REQUIREMENTS OF THE NEW RETRIEVER

Mike realized the new hunting retriever had to have a great race in him. In other words, he had to move—to hunt all day, to cover miles, to not tire or sore-up, to sustain his race.

Therefore, when you go to pick a Lab pup you have an entirely different requirement of physical abilities today than for the old non-slip retrievers who were only released to fetch an upland bird or duck.

Mike realized that what we needed afield was a slightly taller retriever to achieve that kinetic balance necessary for an all-day hunt. A thick, short-legged dog (the old standard) just can't sustain a race, just like the stocky guy is not going to be a miler, not going to be a marathon man. He's going to be pretty fast in a sprint, maybe, but he's just never going to sustain a race.

So to quote Mike: "Consequently the feet became really important. Studying the difference between a hare foot and a cat foot I realized if you get a hare-type foot, you can get all kinds of speed out of the hole, but it's too tiring for a day's run. So you need more of a cat-type foot for the hunting retriever, so it tightens up a little bit and gives the dog the endurance the hunter requires."

Hare and Cat Foot

Now let's analyze these two types of dog feet.

What constitutes a hare foot? Mike tells us, "Look at one of your fingers. From the tip of the nail to the first knuckle is the first joint. A second bone extends from the first joint to the second. And a third bone of that finger extends from the second to the third joint and in a hare foot that bone is significantly longer than in a cat foot. That's what constitutes a hare foot. And a hare foot renders instability. That's right. The center of gravity is too far forward, so the dog continually leans into the race.

"To repeat, a hare foot gives you all kinds of speed out of the hole but it's tiring to get such a long foot going . . . even when swimming.

"So a modified cat foot is much more efficient than a hare foot in an endurance dog. Also, a modified cat foot tightens up a little bit on the run and gives the dog the distance the hunter requires [meaning such a foot is less likely to tire]."

The Forearm

Mike continues, "The length of the forearm is also very important: like in a horse. In fact, a horse's pastern [the part of the foot between the hoof and the fetlock] gives you the proper slope. You want a horse that has a real nice slope to its pastern so his fetlock almost touches the ground when he moves. Because that gives him a shock absorber. It gives him the ability to absorb that jolt; especially in the front.

"And that's just an enormous jolt when the dog is running out there. And that horse's pastern is his shock absorber. And the dogs have to have that same angle. If they're just straight up and down in the front legs, then it's too much shock. By the second morning of a hunt a post-legged dog is so sore he can't hardly run because he's taken such a pounding on his shoulder. You need a dog with that nice slope in his pastern so he can take the shock.

"But at the same time you don't want to get a sloping pastern with a big, long foot (a hare foot). You must have a sloping pastern with a shorter foot and those high toenails. . . . The high toenails are less likely to strike rock and break off. And black ones are tougher, still."

THE RETRIEVER'S NECK

Mike also has thoughts on the retriever's neck. "Now there all types of things that come into play. The length of the neck is very important. I struggled with that for a while. I ended up in my breeding program where the necks got a little bit too long. Yet when I shortened them they got too thick.

"What's involved in the neck is this: if too long, it alters the dog's stability, it provides instability. Let's examine this instability.

"What makes the racehorse run is the instability to the front—leaning forward, he has to continue to run fast or fall down. With this forward thrust, this imbalance, the horse has more power. That's why the workhorse leans into a tight line held by the teamster . . . this gives the horse more instability which provides more power. It moves the center of gravity forward. The most efficient animal is the one that moves his center of gravity in the straightest and flattest line. And that's what we want of our hunting retrievers.

"If a dog is too short, however, the neck gets shorter and broader, which naturally tapers into a large rib cage and that, too, is too much 'proportionate' weight for the running Lab to carry.

"So that rib cage . . . which is determined by the thickness of the neck . . . is proportionately broader. What we really want is depth in the brisket, not width.

"A short, thick neck always provides for a thicker chest. . . . And again that's one of the polygenetic types of traits you won't find on a lean dog.

"So the neck has got to be just the right length to 1) balance the dog,

Two excellent, but seldom seen, retrievers are the Irish water spaniel (left), waiting for Omar Driskill, Simsboro, Louisiana, to throw the duck, and the flat-coated retriever (right) shown posing with a pheasant rooster. (Flat-coat photograph © Bill Marchel)

2) not tip the dog forward, 3) nor be too heavy and end up evolving into a too-heavy chest."

Balance

In addition, Mike says, "a Lab must be in balance to be a good runner or swimmer. A big, block-headed Lab . . . what we used to call cobby . . . is pretty. But today's longer Lab needs a narrower head. Also the tail has to get longer to provide the kinetic balance we want.

"If you have a short-legged Lab in the front, you end up with a chopped gait. That means the dog sores up in the elbows and shoulders. The slope of the shoulder should be greater than 60 percent if the dog is really short and stiff in front. A significant portion of a dog's shock-absorbing ability is provided by his shoulder blades."

Shock Absorbers

"The dog with pitiful shock-absorbing capability," Mike says, "is usually the dog with straight legs [that are] short in front. The paws slam down on each stride. It's unbelievable pressure for both the pasterns and

A dog is a dog: What works for one works for the other. (Photograph © Lon E. Lauber)

shoulder blades.

"Now short legs in back cause a rolling motion, a bouncing motion. It looks like the dog is stubbing its toes and bouncing up in the air in the back.

"You see these dogs: They always look like they're hustling, but they don't get anywhere. That's because the arc of the leg stroke is shortened. And short back legs are much worse in appearance than short front legs. They really do look funny. These dogs seem to hop like a rabbit with both back legs."

The High Tail

Now Mike has a few thoughts about the tail: "I've found if you raise the tail up you get the pleasing appearance in back you seek. Of course . . . a high tail extends the pelvic drive muscles and gives more drive to the wheel of the legs. Too low a tail also gives the dog a rounded-butt look. And this is important. When you see that rounded-butt look in a dog's rear end, you know that dog is not going to have much endurance."

The Coat

"And finally," Mike says, "look at the Lab's coat. Try to find a litter with short, slick coats. Such a dog won't heat up as fast as a long-haired or kinky-haired dog."

Putting Mike's Advice to Good Use

You can gauge what Mike says only by looking at the *parents,* not the pups. You can get a false reading by looking at that roly-poly pup. So you see why it's imperative to get a look at both parents before buying your retriever prospect. And you can learn the most by seeing them run in the field.

Dragging a Rag

You might say, "All you've given us is okay, but you still haven't told us how to pick the right pup from the nest."

Oh, there's all kinds of ploys. This guy takes a pup off by itself to see if it's shy. Or he makes loud noises and sees if one or more pups become alarmed. Some lady may drag a rag around to see which pups give chase. Or another may produce a bird wing to see what dog will freeze at attention.

All this goes on and on. But recently at one of our gun dog group workshops I asked this very question—about picking a pup—and was pleased when there was consensus. Can you figure what all the pros agreed on?

Well, it was this: Pick the pup that picks you.

This makes an awful lot of sense, for later you're going to learn that pups and dogs have extrasensory perception (ESP). In other words, pups and dogs can read our mind, and they can do so with many miles between the communicating parties.

What's likely is the pup who picks you has already gauged your inner self and feels the two of you can make a go of it. This explanation is good enough for me, and I've spent a lifetime trying to understand what's going on between a human and a dog.

Permit Me a Word

I've said nothing about retriever breeds: flat-coat, Lab, golden, Chesie, curly-coat, plus American and Irish water spaniels. In great part their differences are irrelevant to me; a dog is a dog and a retriever is a retriever.

I've had as many as thirty personal dogs back on the farm, not counting clients and dogs in training. Of the thirty I usually kept, some eighteen would be Labs. And there wasn't much about their breed they didn't reveal to me. But there were other breeds as well. I was training cattle dogs, sheep dogs, personal protection dogs, and scent-discrimination dogs. There were the obedience classes and the agility work and all of it. If it was doggy, I did it or am doing it. That's my life, my love, and my dedication.

So when I talk of a Shih Tzu, I'm talking of a Lab, an Irish wolfhound, a spitz, or a Chihuahua. A dog is a dog. Oh, there are minute differences: the innate tenacity of an English bulldog, the grit of an Australian shepherd, the brilliance of a border collie, the mellowness of a Lab, the possessiveness of a Chesie. But that doesn't negate the fact that each of these breeds—and all others—have similar physiologies, psychological predispositions, and natural inclinations.

And having said that I want you to know there can be more differences *within* a breed than *between* two breeds. That's because of haphazard breeding.

If you want to play favorites, then go ahead. My job here is to train

Pick the pup that picks you. (Photograph © Mark Kayser)

whatever you pick, whatever you have. Permit me that, okay? For the system I present here does a crackerjack job with all of them.

IF PUP PICKED YOU

So we've considered the essentials in picking a pup. But what would the pup look for if he was picking you? Worth thinking about, isn't it? Would you qualify as a prospective partner?

Well, let's get to preparing our home and our life for Pup.

Turn the page.

③

House Fit for a Dog

"The best dog house for your dog is the one you live in."
—Author

Okay, you've made your decision and handed over the cash, and Pup's in a cardboard box in the back seat as you head home. If you've made the right choice, Pup has climbed out of his box by now, fallen on the floor, and is bawling like a banshee. Every pup that escaped the box on me turned out to be a good one.

So reach back and pick him up, put him on your lap, rub those velvet ears, and wait for a warm moisture to permeate your jeans as you think of this:

Having got a pup, enjoy it. Be done with all that demanding and corralling and suppressing that the pros usually practice and the books preach. Let the pup have his head, his life, and you go along for the fun. And never look at the clock—let Pup set his own pace. And hopefully he's afield with you, let's say, three days a week.

Also, if you really want to consider serious training, then train Pup yourself. Only a few pups are born with a behavioral fault. For the most part, that's all plastered on by the human partner: even the hidden balks. So be careful what you teach and how you teach. Make sure you've got the smarts and temperament to do it right.

PUP AND THE PACK
Let's get Pup started on the right foot. If you have dogs waiting at home,

---

When guests enter our home they are told, "This is the dogs' house. This is their furniture. You may use it if you want, but they may join you. That's their right." (Photograph © Marilyn "Angel" Wynn)

then carry the brand new pup in your arms and walk out into the back-yard, let's say. All the dogs are going to gather and leap and try to decode what you're carrying.

When the pandemonium is somewhat manageable, lower Pup to the grass. All the dogs will close in and nose him. Never again can I imagine a pup being more intimidated. But here's what I hope you see. It's been my ecstasy to envision a rocket exploding in air as the strident strains of a military march comes to my ear, and the little pup wedges his way through the mob, carrying a tattered battle flag, as he leaves all the klutzes standing and dumbfoundedly sniffing. If so, you've got a good one.

However, if the pup does go down (folds), gently scoop him up, cooing to him and then, nestled warmly and firmly in your cupped palms, show him to the pack. We're going to get through this one way or the other, and Pup is not going to be frightened by this gang.

Soon you can lower him again and all will go well. But the dogs will still pester him if he stoops to tinkle. Tinkling is mighty big for any dog, so monitor.

FEEDING

One other time they'll show interest in him will be at dinner time. Dogs are natural food thieves. They think all food should be theirs.

Therefore, it is imperative Pup be guarded each time he eats. And he must always eat in the same place (hopefully at the same time). There'll be meals he has no appetite, so this routine can require some effort on your part while guarding him.

Each marauding dog must be told this is Pup's place, so bug off. It'll take time, but soon it will stick. Then, note this, all dogs will respect Pup's plate as long as he stands over it. Dogs are like that. They honor food so much they'll not try to steal so long as any dog continues to eat his or her own meal. But let that dog walk away, and the pack will vie for the remnants. Also, keep the puppy away from all other dogs' plates. They'll growl for sure and maybe snap.

Oh, there are exceptions to this, but there are exceptions to every-thing. I have one dog who delights in leaving some morsels on her plate so some other dog can come and stick a hopeful nose in while the pos-sessor gives a long, low growl. This is her daily delight. Every dog has some favorite game.

All gun dogs must either live in your house, or should they live in a kennel, they must be invited inside each night. (Photograph © Jim Ruppel)

The House Inside the House

It's imperative you have an airline crate waiting for Pup. The crate is used to give Pup a place of his own, keep him from tearing up the house, and prompt him to dump outside. He sleeps in the crate all night and that solves one problem. But when he's awake you must monitor him carefully.

For Pup's comfort throw a pad or blanket in that crate. Give some luxury, and don't think pups can't tell the difference between satin and burlap.

A dog doesn't want to mess its nest, so make sure the crate fits the pup's size. If the nest is too large, Pup can go to a far corner and break his inherited predisposition. You know, the pup figures, "I've got acres; a little mess way over there really doesn't qualify as being in my nest over here." To train a dog you've got to know dogs—know how they're built and how they think.

The airline crate for safekeeping and housebreaking.

TINKLING AND DUMPING

After each feeding Pup must be taken outside while you stand and wait and encourage and finally praise him, for, "Ya did a good job!"

But that's not all: It's necessary you take Pup to the same place each time since pups are very place conscious. It won't be long before he recognizes that patch of yard as his dump area.

Watch Pup's behavior in the house. He'll send definite clues. Should he suddenly take off running for no apparent reason, with no apparent destination, get him outside. Or, if he starts going in circles, rush him outdoors.

When Pup graduates from the crate to run-of-the-house you'll need a doggy door. Why? Have you ever danced outside a locked bathroom door while your fifteen-year-old daughter suffered death throes because she found a pimple on her chin?

BONDING

Now during all of this when Pup's at foot and elbow he learns the

Seven-week-old yellow Labs socializing and bonding. (Photograph © Lon E. Lauber)

territory and you. Pup sees you in every position, every mood, every circumstance. He learns to read your most subtle nuance, which results in his knowing you.

And if you think about it, to really know someone is to owe someone. For you build up an inventory of needs and duties and expectations. And that's called bonding, which is sharing one soul, one heart, one psyche. The dog grows to need the human, and the human seeks ways to repay the kid-in-the-fur-coat for being a good dog.

When Pup Enters the House

Awhile back we were introducing Pup to the house pack. Now we take him inside and let him down. Let him roam, sniff, poke into dark recesses. Do not inhibit him. This house is his and he must have that feeling. If you want him in a doghouse out back, then I ask you to consider the possibility of you and he ever bonding. Put your spouse in a little house out there and see how life goes. Okay?

Pup-Proof the Place

Now Pup can get killed in your place. So unplug all electrical wires accessible to him. Keep all cupboard doors closed—we don't want him into poisons. Also watch carefully what's laying around that he can ingest. A pup can swallow a man's sock and require stomach surgery.

Also, Pup can destroy possessions of yours to the point where you'd want to kill him. Fringe on table spreads and rugs are irresistible. Shoes are ice cream, as are underwear. Wooden legs on all furniture beckons the chewer. Keep a close eye.

But there are aids for the hard-pressed home keeper. Like Bitter Apple. Just spray those wood legs with Bitter Apple, and Pup will leave them alone. Or use pepper spray—that works, too.

You've just got to be conscientious, for I don't want your chance to develop a great gun dog dashed over some damned table leg. And that can happen. One maniacal act on your part can put Pup down forever. He will never trust you again.

The Experimental Dog

All my dogs are experiments. There's so much I need to learn. So I come upon odd dogs and bring them home. In other words, I deny all the good sense I preach to you. For example, I've learned the best age to bring a

You need to pup-proof your place; anything left laying around is a potential chew toy. (Photograph © Jack Macfarlane Photography)

pup home for me—not necessarily for you, understanding you have other dogs in residence—is *four or five weeks.* Now let me explain.

Why do I specify other dogs aboard? Simple. A dog must learn to be a dog. If you have no dogs on the premises, then wait until Pup is at least seven weeks so he'll have had the opportunity to "become a dog" in the litter.

The point then is a four-or-five-week-old pup must be socialized by both humans and dogs. Both people and dogs contribute their specificity to the Pup's eventual mental health, sense of being, self-confidence, and excellence as a companion.

But I have known of five-week-old pups adjusting without dogs in the new home.

THE OLD PUP

I mention this because I'll bring home pups of all ages.

And where you really get into trouble is with a three-month-old pup, the very age you find so many mall pups, since they're usually not shipped to the store until seven weeks of age, and the shop hasn't been able to sell them.

Well, a pup that old has already developed a concrete mindset. It will seldom be altered. Take Molly, for instance. I brought Molly, a Pekingese, home at three months. She had been abused by teenage boys in her former home, bullied by the pack, ignored by the rest of the household, and left bored in a sterile backyard. She took up eating feces.

THE EXCEPTION

With all the negative things that happened to Molly, she showed her abuse with a trembling tail. Every time you looked at Molly and said her name, her uncertainty showed by her trembling tail. No matter the love and assurance my wife, Dee, and I give to Molly, there's always that tremor to her tail, always that drop of acid in her stomach, that signal of uncertainty.

Also, anytime a teenage boy comes around, Molly folds.

And yes, we stopped the coprophagy by sheer diligence; we kept the backyard picked up so there was no temptation. Then through encouragement and discipline, Molly gave up the disgusting practice.

A PUP IS A SLATE: BE CAREFUL WHAT YOU WRITE

What I want you to realize is Pup is a slate: Everything that happens in his life—especially his first seven weeks—leaves a message. Bad message. Good message. And the longer the pup is left with the breeder and the litter, the greater a chance a bad message is going to be written.

You'll never know what went on. Neighbors, the breeder's family, prospective buyers, the trip to the vet for puppy shots—who knows who did what?

Now, in my house, I know everything that happens is gauged to help Pup. So I want him with me. Understand? The damage is done for Molly; she is doomed to gulp every time someone notices her.

And never again, in all of any pup's life, will it be as pliable, as impressionable, as receptive, as keenly attentive as during that period between four and seven weeks. I mean it. I can't put a definite figure on it, but possibly 95 percent of everything Pup will ever be is formed within the first forty-nine days.

SCOTT AND PFAFFENBERGER

Greater minds than mine have determined this.

The two most brilliant and influential dog scientists in the twentieth century were Peter Scott and Clarence Pfaffenberger. They lived in an overload mode of complex pup research. Pfaffenberger was the wizard who forged the Guide Dogs for the Blind training and breeding program. Dr. Scott was closely associated with the Roscoe B. Jackson Memorial Laboratory in Bar Harbor, Maine, where he sought insight into the cause of problems in children by monitoring puppies and dogs in controlled situations.

Pfaffenberger first came to my attention in San Rafael, California, where pioneers and philanthropists saw the need to provide Seeing Eye dogs for returning World War II veterans who were blind. Pfaffenberger also contributed to Scott's research at Bar Harbor.

Pfaffenberger's goal was to perfect the ideal pup for guide dog work, which meant a dog that could be trained to assist any blind person—a life and death responsibility.

The guide dog program was such a success that by 1984 the staff was disappointed if one dog failed from each litter. And that is amazing; that is identical to a gun dog man breeding up a line of Labs where each pup became a master hunter (and I mean in the field and not a test hunt).

While Pfaffenberger was juggling all these projects, Peter Scott was discovering what he would later label "the critical periods in a puppy's life." He learned that pups in a litter could learn specific things at specific times during maturation. Furthermore, Scott learned if a pup didn't learn any one hoped-for behavior at the optimum time, chances were he'd never learn it. This means the raising of a litter is a very critical and very important undertaking that requires constant vigilance and dedication from the breeder.

Now the first conclusion that came from these two men's research was this: The ideal time to adopt a pup is seven weeks. The point being, the pup has been socialized and conditioned by the litter and the breeder, and is now physically and psychologically ready for both the new human partner and the world.

The essential difference between Scott and Pfaffenberger and myself is I've chosen five weeks as the ideal adoption age—that is if there are dogs in the home. You do what you please.

I've just traveled too many thousand miles gathering dog stories for *Field & Stream* and met too many thousand dogs and owners who have found that the younger the adopted pup, the better the grown dog.

THE FOUR-WEEK-OLD PUP NAMED SPORT

One case in point. Thomas Newton, a rustic, backwoods traditionalist who lived until 1997 on a patch of south-central Tennessee farmland with his wife, Hazel, once brought home a four-week-old setter pup (the mother had died).

It was winter so Thomas put the pup in a box behind the wood stove, then went out and milked a cow so the pup could eat.

Thomas was not a dog trainer. Matter of fact, in the old days hardly anyone was a dog trainer. The dog just lived with the human companions. You know, plowed with them, planted with them, harvested with them, fished with them, went to town with them, then lo and behold, went hunting with them.

Well, Sport—that was the name Thomas gave the pup—became a heroic figure in those parts. He could provide you a dinner of beaver, opossum, raccoon, turkey, squirrel, bobwhite, ducks, geese. Whataya want? Sport would go get it.

And I've seen this very set of facts over and over.

HE JUST GOES WITH ME EVERYWHERE I GO

You all know the story I tell in about every book I write about the sheep

The most impressionable age for pups is from three to seven weeks. (Photograph © Mark Kayser)

You will have much more difficulty bonding with a pup left alone until twelve weeks or older. (Photograph © William H. Mullins)

herder I met while backpacking with my Labs. He had a nine-month-old border collie that was phenomenal. This dog could probably mine gold, run a computer, build an adobe hut, you know?

So I told the shepherd, "You must be quite a trainer." And he said back, "Me a trainer? No way. The dog just goes with me wherever I go." So you see why Pup must be in the house? He must be in your life. You don't train great dogs, you just let them grow up with you, loving them every moment of the day.

And they train themselves.

Now let me put all this in perspective.

Pfaffenberger tells us in his book *The New Knowledge of Dog Behavior* that the truth of the data they collected leads them to assume that leaving a puppy in a kennel for more than two weeks with no dog or human contact, or to break off socialization which has been conducted for, let's say, a period of just one day a week for five weeks, will greatly decrease the trainability of the pup when it attains adulthood.

The point is this: *The litter-box life of a pup must provide maximum stimuli from both canine and human sources.* And this stimulus enrichment must be constant and uninterrupted. *The period between three weeks, when the pups open their eyes, until seven weeks, when the pup's brain reaches the final stage of physical development, constitutes the most impressionable, most molding, most behavior-forming, most critical, and most permanent determinant of Pup's life.*

Also, the litter-box pup's capability of total absorption of new stimuli persists from seven weeks to twelve weeks, and from then on it moderates until learning becomes slow going. The fact is all of the first three months of Pup's life are the developmental months, but in the latter part of this period and later, the human relationship has a decreasing effect on the socialization of the pup.

Now any pup will love you if you're his source of life and joy from five to seven weeks. But that same pup left alone until it is twelve weeks old will seldom give its body and soul to anyone. But all rules can be overruled, in this case by sensitive training. In the case of Molly, her response to the special treatment she's received from Dee and me has her coming for love, assurance, and a sense of anchoring.

You can almost say what happens during the twenty-one days between four weeks old and seven weeks old determines what Pup will become—good or bad—forever, for that good or bad can never be altered except by exceptional sensitivity and total commitment on the part of a trainer.

So Much To Say All at Once

I bought Sugar, a Lhasa apso, on a Monday, saw a doctor on a Tuesday, and was told I had a blood clot in my right leg and to go home and sit down with the leg propped up for thirty days.

So Sugar and I sat for thirty days.

Little did I know what was happening. But nine years later Sugar has never been out of my shadow. During those thirty days—which was her sixth to tenth week—Sugar imprinted on me like I was the air she had to breathe, like we were joined at the hip. And no matter what excitement is happening to the rest of the household—let's say Dee has found a new treat and is handing it out in the kitchen—Sugar will not leave my side.

Such devotion is very humbling, and it is a great responsibility. I've been told everyone in the house feels Sugar is going to die each time I leave town. The heart that pumps for her is not inside her, it has left town with me.

Maybe now you can see the total impact a human can have on a pup just by having it in company all the time.

The Scuttled Lab

Nearly forty years ago I bought a two-year-old Lab called Renegade Pepe. I bought him on a contract that said I'd pay a bonus when Pepe made his amateur or open field championship. Field trials weren't so bad then, and electric collars had not been distributed for general use. And trainers who proceeded by pain had to get off their butts and run or swim the errant pooch down.

Pepe had tons of potential but was dry-docked at two. Why? Due to training difficulties, Pepe would not enter the water. Think of that, a Lab who wouldn't go to sea.

Well, my program was to *love* Pepe to water. I started in the summer and went in a bathing suit to our club training pond. Pepe sat on shore and stared at me.

I took bread with me, and, since bread floats, I pinched off bits and tossed them toward shore. Pepe, who loved to eat, said, "A dog does not live by bread alone," and stayed put.

When winter came I was still wet and Pepe was dry. By then I was in the pond in waders.

By the following spring—with the help of a fabulous duck season that drew Pepe to water since he couldn't resist live game—we were ready for the field trial circuit. Within two months I had to hand over the bonus. Pepe was a champion. And realize: Once again it took a bird to train a bird dog.

So please note here: 1) full commitment, 2) patience, 3) perseverance, 4) love, and 5) birds, are some of the imperatives to training that retriever you just bought.

Now you can't say I was "training" Pepe. There were no drills, no point of contact. You could say I was bonding with him, restoring his confidence in himself, showing him I'd ask nothing of him that I wouldn't do, proving water never hurt anyone, and when the ducks came, letting him learn just how exciting hunting was.

Why Train At All?

But there's more than that. I'm almost to the point where I reject training per se. It can be rigid, dull, intimidating, and a wedge to be driven between you and Pup. I have now proven, and it has been proven to me by others, that the primary requirement in bringing along a dog is time spent together and total commitment.

I believe there is an osmosis, a permeation of the dog's psyche and soul that eases through, migrates through, filters through—hell, I don't know—where the dog learns to perceive your intent and performs to please you. And this is hundreds of times more powerful than training.

I have seen this too many times. A pup can see the discipline trainer as a frowning face, a punitive voice, an intimidating posture, the foot tread too quick and intolerant, the hand too heavy and fast. The trainer honestly doesn't know he's conveying all these threats. So that's why I'd prefer that Pup not be trained at all.

ESP

How else could Mike Gould cast Web over a hill—with the wind blowing over Web and toward Mike—and silently, Mike would step forward and Web would go back. Mike would back up and Web would come in. Mike would walk right and Web would go left. And Mike would walk left and Web would go right.

Matter of fact, Mike says the human's eyes control the dog, even when the dog can't see your face.

I have proven this: Never take your eyes off the dog and it will never veer from your intention. In that regard how many of you have taken your eyes off Pup while he is fetching a bird only to have him stop and tinkle, or drop the bird and wander off, or just change directions and go where he wants?

The eye is an invisible check cord.

Web, quite frankly, was reading Mike's mind on the other side of the hill—he was using ESP over a long distance. It is said ancient man used to have this faculty but relinquished it. Well, dogs have kept it keen, they can do it, and they do do it.

Another story.

Jack Robinson of Dayton, Tennessee, is a member of the National Bird Dog Championship board of directors and a clothing manufacturer. His office is festooned with Field Trial Hall of Fame certificates his dogs have won.

Now Jack's big-time bird dogs are bred and trained to run—after all, they are hunted off horseback. Yet Jack tells us, regarding their offspring, "If you can start those pups as early as seven weeks, and you've got a place where you can walk them and fool with them and get them to come back to you, then that's the way to do it.

"Don't let that puppy lay in a kennel until he's six months old [which used to be the practice] before you turn him loose. If you do, his natural breeding and instinct is going to produce a dog that runs long through the country looking for birds. Therefore, the primary thing you must teach is for the pup to come back to you."

YOUNG AND IMPRESSIONABLE

There it is again. When that pup is impressionable, eager, and full of zest, give him your life. Give him your time and commitment. And that pup will bond with you and spend the rest of his life trying to please you, for making you happy will become the most important thing in that pup's life.

NEVER BE RIGID

Now another thought.

Several years ago some books came out alluding to Peter Scott and concentrating on "critical times in a puppy's maturation," that is, when

Getting your retriever pup to eat dinner is generally not a problem. (Photograph © Gary Kramer)

Pup could learn. Well, the results were disastrous. Puppy owners interpreted the material with *rigid perspective* then became alarmed when Pup, let's say, didn't sit up on the forty-ninth day.

Dog pros across the nation were plagued with frantic inquiries about, "Why can't my dog fetch? She's fifty-six days old; we're falling way behind." And when the pups were actually delivered to the pros for correction, it was found the animal had been scuttled.

You don't train a pup with a clock, nor do you attempt to make Pup fit a rigid system. No science of training a pup can ever approximate the *art* of getting the job done. For dog training is a matter of the heart, not a calculator.

Consequently, every fact I present must be tempered with the reality of your personality, Pup's personality, the capability of both of you, including what is your experience, your intent, and your expectations.

Got it?

Plus, I've never read a canine researcher who addressed three pivotal realities. One, they never discuss bonding. This is the power base of any dog/human relationship, as evidenced by Sugar. And two, they seemingly downplay the power of scent over all other canine faculties. Plus, I've read entire gun dog training books that have never mentioned a bird.

We won't do that.

Now we know that environment and genetic predisposition determine Pup's life. But in that environment you are an entity.

And you constitute what? Some 90 percent of it all?

I'm saying that without the very many years of combined dog training experience Dee and I have, Molly would never have become a pleasurable dog. And she is. She's absolutely a delight.

I just brought home a five-week-old Shih Tzu pup we named Cookie. Cookie has a big motor in her two-pound body, a hot temper, an athlete's balance and determination, plus a desire to run the show. Well, Molly adopted Cookie, raised her, schooled her, and formed her into a pleasant ten-pound member of the pack. No one could have done it better. It's like Molly was saying, "What happened to me is not going to happen to you."

TIME FOR DINNER

Nutritionists abound, so pay heed to what they say. That's their business. Me? I never took a canine dietary course in my life. I've just raised several hundred pups and know what worked for me.

Get some powdered milk, some puppy kibbles, and some canned meat formulated for puppies. If you want to be heavy on the meat, then do it. If you want to be heavy on the kibbles, do it. The amount of water will determine the consistency of your gruel. Plus, it will soften those kibbles so a small mouth with baby jaws can handle them.

Test your offering. Pup may want it watery or thick, warm or cold. Feed three times a day for three months, then go to twice a day for two years. You may then drop to one meal a day if you wish, but I always stay at two half servings because dogs love food so much.

I've also tried self-feeding Labs from a gravity-flow container. If the dog's a hog, you'll have a fat dog. Assuredly we must balance food intake with exercise. Hyper young gun dogs can run all day and burn the calories. But old, lay-about seniors take it easy and need little fuel. Feed accordingly.

PROTEIN

When Pup's two years old, taper off protein (read your label for the percentage of protein). For protein can kill a dog. I seek protein in the realm of 5 percent during non-hunting season. Most dry foods are around 22 percent. That's too much protein for my liking, even when Pup's hunting hard.

You must know there are three primary causes of canine death (in this order): cancer, heart disease, and kidney failure. Protein enhances kidney failure.

And a final word about protein and kidneys: Because pups are born with 65 to 75 percent more kidney than they need, a great amount of kidney damage can occur before tests show Pup's in danger. You usually find out too late.

SHOULD YOU SPAY OR NEUTER?

Well, we could go on and on. But we've got Pup pretty well settled in your home.

Many decisions I leave for you. If you want to spay or neuter, have at it. No way does it alter Pup's behavior. You do have to be aware of weight gain, however.

It is difficult to have a house bitch in heat. The spotting gets old and cleaning it off gets tedious. But those are personal decisions for you only.

CLEANING UP

What goes in must come out. And not always in the right place. Therefore, Pup will have a bowel or bladder accident in your house. Don't panic. Worse yet, don't go charging the dog, for there are solvents and cleaners on the market that make sopping up a cinch.

Let me interrupt. Thoughtful potty training can save a pup. Fitful nagging and raging tantrums will destroy him—forever. Which of us can recall the mistakes we presented our folks? Were we beat for those transgressions, screamed at, snatched up and thrown into the yard? If so, we're probably reading this book in some state penitentiary or a psychiatrist's office, for with treatment like that we undoubtedly got screwed up and everything went wrong.

As for cleaning up, nothing works better than simple vinegar and water. Pad wet spots dry with paper towels or rags, pressing out all dampness. Then spray and scrub with vinegar water. Nothing to it.

Number two? Just pick up and flush. Treat any dampness as you would tinkle. Now the worst spot of all is the color yellow, like yellow bile upchuck. Get on it fast. I mean fast. Or it will prove indelible on some carpet fabrics. Saturate a large towel and scrub, or get a bottle of water and just flood the area. Then scrub and dry.

When all else fails buy or rent an electric carpet cleaner. I've got a Bissel Big Green, which is the best buy I think I ever made. I've never seen anything work as good in my life. Matter of fact, get a carpet cleaner on a yellow stain within five minutes and when everything dries you can't find the spot.

WHOSE HOUSE IS IT?

Too many dog people don't give their dogs the run of their house. I've often wondered why. In their mind is the dog some sort of servant instead of a family member? You know, the dog is there to baby-sit, guard the place, get the bird, win the ribbon—for me!

My wife and I have never taken in a dog for those reasons. We have an entirely different kind of hope: We pray the dogs will love us and make us happy and healthy and give us something to care for. And we further pray that we can provide them benefit equal to what they give us: lowering our incidence of disease by 75 percent and cutting our prescription needs in half (these two facts have just been reported by a Boston care center with full-time, live-in dogs).

Pup's attention span is short, so training sessions must be short too. The key to success is to work in many short sessions instead of a few long ones. (Photograph © William H. Mullins)

This Chesie pup gets early knowledge of ducks in addition to spending the day with the handler.

When guests enter our home they are told, "This is the dogs' house. This is their furniture. You may use it if you want, but they may join you. That's their right."

No Time Out

What's really important in Pup's life is this. Say you want to adopt a pup, really got your heart set on it. But you're going to take a three-week business trip, or you have a baby sitter and you and your spouse are off on a two-week cruise. Well, don't get Pup.

You've got to have constant contact. You've got to fill every moment of his life. For everything that happens during those early weeks is levered. Those early weeks are thousands of times more important than the weeks you spend with Pup when he is nine months old.

And I'm not talking just house time. You've got to be afield with Pup. You've got to have made prior arrangement to get him into birds. I mean birds at five weeks. For you can't train a bird dog without a bird, and

Pup's never going to have such a grasping mind as those first few weeks.

Bird association for a seven-week-old pup is 50, 100, 1,000 times more impressionable, exciting, memorable, challenging, and destiny-fulfilling than at any later time.

But know this. Pup's attention span, at best, is fifteen minutes, let's say. So that means you've got to work in as many fifteen-minute sessions a day as you can. Any time longer than this is tedium for Pup—boredom, dumdum, dullsville, and actually counterproductive.

Also, I have this warning—and it is a real warning—and you must take heed.

THE WEEK OF SUICIDE

When Pup enters the ninth week he thinks he's Superdog. I mean it. He will leap from a ledge ten times his height, try to leap from one surface to another though they may be eight feet apart. You really have to think for Pup during this ninth week.

By the tenth week the insanity is gone. Now, if anything, Pup is spooked. Too many accidents in the ninth week, I guess. But I warn you, you can lose Pup during the ninth week if you don't keep him from committing suicide.

THE NEXT CHAPTER

Continuing to understand and do our best with Pup, let's have one more chapter on puppies. Only this time, what happens to Pup is beyond our control. There are things the breeder should be doing. If he doesn't it won't hurt you, but if he does it will help.

Read on.

4

Training Pup From Womb to One Year

"Little by little [Jock, the dog] got into the way of imitating all I did, so that after a while it was hardly necessary to say a word or make a sign to him. He lay down beside me and raised his head to look, just as he saw me do."
—Sir Percy Fitzpatrick, *Jock of the Bushveld*

At no time in any living thing's life is he or she more comfortable or more well tended than in the womb, with its constant temperature, continual nourishment, complete protection, total blanketing, the reassuring throb of the heartbeat, and the mother's voice.

Yes, the mother's voice, which I'll explain in a minute, and most certainly her heart. For what puppy is not put to sleep by the metronome ticking of a clock? Or a baby, suckling its mother's breast, with its ear near her heart—a throbbing sound the baby has heard during gestation? For a pup or a human baby both remember their mother's heartbeat, have it memorized, and know it means total protection and contentment.

At no time has this fetal training been made more apparent to me than when my friend Steve Kaufman, a computer wizard who lives in Sedona, Arizona, last visited me to remove the agonies I've placed in my computer.

IT'S FOR THE BIRDS

Steve brought along his bird family: one sun conure parrot and two cockatiels. I sat next to the cockatiels' cage and listened to them sing and talk to their eggs. Yes, they knew those peeps inside could hear them. Steve,

An adolescent black Lab with a wing. (Photograph © Bill Buckley/The Green Agency)

who is a bird expert, says at no other time do they talk and sound so sweetly. "It's a totally different sound," he says. "It's special."

Then he floored me by relating, "All birds talk to their eggs."

I then remembered the movie *Fly Away Home,* in which the human father and daughter guide the flying geese from Canada to Dixie by leading the way in their respective ultralights. At the start of that movie some recording instruments zeroed in on several goose eggs, and you could hear the unborn goslings talking. To whom? Just talking—that's the point. Were they talking to their mother? She surely talked to them as their bodies developed. They knew her voice; she now knows theirs. It's just fascinating.

Anyway, I now know that among certain (and maybe all) living species, there is cross-placenta communication.

A human's voice (especially a man's) can cause a slight rise in the rate of a pup's fetal heartbeat, while at the same time, the pup's mother's voice will slow down that rate. This perhaps offers something to clarify why women make the best puppy trainers.

COMMUNICATING WITH THE FETAL PUP

So what I'm leading up to is communicating with pups in the embryo. Or, more precisely, training pups in the womb. This is one of Gary Ruppel's specialties. Gary is a Kiowa, Colorado, do-it-all gun dog pro who teaches pointers to fetch, retrievers to point, and all other gun dogs to do what they regularly do. In other words, Gary is a traditionalist, plus an innovator, and has both success and fun at being versatile.

He's also very unique, since he trains with genuine, unconditional love. Gary has told me, "If I get a client's dog in here who doesn't like me—and I always can tell—it really upsets me and I get to work to win over that dog's friendship. I sit down with that dog and I tell him, 'Look, we're in this thing together. Right off I liked you. Would you please try to like me?'"

Unlike Gary, many pros training in America would get that same dog in, see his indifference or surliness, and say, "Who gives a damn?" then start manhandling. You and I know a few, and among the rest we can conjecture. You know it takes a lot more patience and commitment to sit down and talk to a dog, physically stroke him, genuinely inquire about his well being (and yes, dogs know genuineness when they hear it), than to haul off and hit the dog in the head with a club or shock him with a

Maximize Pup's fetching instinct by accepting anything Pup brings you, limbs and all.
(Photograph © Gary Kramer)

cattle prod, and yell, "Damn it, you'll do it or else."

In this light, I want to again bring in Bob Wehle, who is a delightful force in humane gun dog training. Bob is a gentleman, a scholar, a substantial businessman, and a master of many arts and trades.

In his book *Snakefoot: The Making of a Champion,* Bob mentions two of his trainers, Chester and Ella Shultz at Bob's New York kennels. Bob writes, and this is so important to support what Gary's doing plus what I wrote in the prologue about trainers being helpmates and buddies, "The personalities and friendliness of my adult dogs I attribute to Ella's humanizing them from day one."

Train, Pain, Disdain

I once knew a man with thunderclouds in his head, who delighted in muscling his dogs. At a pond one day, he put his Lab on the dam, applied a half nelson around its right, upper leg, and broke the dog's shoulder. Yep, that's training.

I bought the dog so it could escape from this man, and I gave it free roam of the farm for the rest of its life.

Whistle Training

Gary Ruppel's the type who would have done the same thing that I did for such a dog.

Gary has his kennels and training grounds right on his home place, which is situated on rural acreage, so he's at the kennels every day. Gary wears a braided lanyard with a couple of small pea whistles that he blows constantly.

Any pregnant bitch, her puppies, and all the dogs who either belong to Gary or are there in training hear this whistle as often each day as they feel the Rocky Mountain's east rampart winds.

Gary, and many other trainers, also pipe constant music into the kennels. It soothes and relaxes the dogs.

But the whistle—all the rest of that dog's life he is going to hear that whistle any time something pleasant happens to him: feed/whistle, birds/whistle, take a swim/whistle, run in the fields as a pack/whistle.

A psychologist would call this "total conditioning." That is, the whistle is a signal that triggers a response. And in this case, the dog is already doing something that pleases him, then Gary's whistle reinforces this gratification.

The dogs recall that a whistle attends every pleasure they know. So why not hike up their attitude? The whistle says things are great. And so it goes.

These dogs have been buttressed, they know things are going to be good, so they are up when Gary releases one for training, and bingo! the dog nails the test. Knowing he has succeeded, the dog returns to the kennel to heighten the expectations of the rest of the dogs—for they sense his success—and they, too, excel.

And that's dog training.

WEHLE AGAIN

Bob Wehle has a different approach. He carries a goose horn with him when making his rounds of the puppy kennels. Yes, Bob has a big operation. In searching for the ultimate gun dog (English pointer) he'll whelp, say, 150 pups a year.

These little guys are kenneled in a separate part of the kennel complex. Here comes Bob with his horn, which you can hear all over the place.

"Ker . . . runk," it squawks, "ker . . . runk."

All the pups run to Bob, as the distant all-age dogs and derby prospects let it out. "Wow, wow, wow . . . ." They remember their childhood. Bob carries pocket treats, some kind of kibble, and gives each pup a morsel. They are overjoyed. They love the excitement of the horn, Bob's frequent visits, the tussle they have vying with each other for space at the fence. Once again, we're talking about sensitivity training, like I promise in the prologue.

Furthermore, Bob tells us in *Snakefoot*, "Where it all begins is in the whelping box. When a bitch whelps, as the pups come, we place them in an incubator, always leaving [a pup] with the mother to ease her nervousness." Again we see caregiving conscientiousness: giving the mother a thought-out delivery procedure. Everything's based on no-stress. That's the new way of gun dog training.

THE LOSS OF LIBERTY

No living thing likes to give up its freedom. Matter of fact, that may be the biggest fight man ever has—that first time he's told he can or can't do something, especially when there's a point of contact to enforce the order.

"Joy is my quest," says a Lab pup savoring his first duck fetched.

Well, with the most sensitive approach to dog training, nevertheless, we may have to tell Pup heel, sit, stay, come, go, no, and his name as commands.

Well, who wants all the grudge Pup can work up vented against a human? Why not let other dogs take on part of this enforcement job?

But then, let's remember, you, as the puppy buyer, can't do any of this. This must be done by the breeder. All that whistling Gary does and the attachment and maintenance of check cords in the litter box—that's all in the breeder's hands.

And why this puppy check cord? One day you will extend the litter box check cord to a training check cord that Pup will drag during the early stages of his field training. He'll not object to this hindrance; he'll remember he became accustomed to it and it didn't hurt him back in the litter box.

We'll explain how to use the litter box check cord in a minute.

Seven Weeks of Miracles

For now let's catalog the rapid sequence of anatomical, psychological, and behavioral developments that occur during Pup's first seven weeks, when he's cared for by the breeder.

Dr. Jacob Mosier, professor emeritus at Kansas State University, whose academic life was spent primarily studying how best to keep puppies alive from birth to adoption, has told me, "All puppies are born three weeks premature." What he means by this is they are helpless: They can't walk, they can't see, their hearing is feeble, and they can but nuzzle for love and search for Mom's nipples.

Nature's reason for this is that wolves, the ancestors of dogs, were beasts of prey. Genetically, then, the dog mother is also a carnivore and burdened to hunt and kill and fetch food for her young. If pregnant those last three weeks, she'd be handicapped in her quest. By birthing the pups while they are still helpless, she can leave them and know they are not going to stray, as she travels more efficiently (no longer pregnant) on the hunt. Therefore, all pups are born three weeks premature, so Momma can catch enough for herself and her litter to eat. Momma-wolf eats her kill and returns to regurgitate it for the pups.

The mother's oral feeding, more than anything else, makes a pup mouth-oriented. Ever after, any loving of the muzzle by the trainer is a pleasure to the dog. And you know how they lick you as a sign of affection? That is an extension of their cleaning off the mouth whiskers of mother at feed time. And what is it dogs love more than food? Nothing.

PUP'S MATURATION
The way it goes:

> First Two Weeks: Pup crawls, nurses, seeks warmth of litter, needs anal stimulation for urination and defecation.
>
> Two Weeks to Three Weeks: Eyes open, teeth appear; Pup stands on four legs, begins to lap liquids, defecates without mother's stimulation; beginning of pack-oriented behavior.
>
> Three Weeks to Five Weeks: Pup can hear, begins to eat food, starts to bark, wag tail, bite littermates, bares teeth, growls, chews, plays prey-killing games. Central nervous system develops rapidly; Pup begins acquiring a sense of distance, and when a pup visibly reacts to all loud sounds, he is starting his socialization stage. If during this period the pup is never roughed up by his littermates and fights back, investigates his surroundings, is relieved of all stress, and has all needs met before they even occur to him, he will remain a perpetual pup for the rest of his life. See why you must have other dogs at home for a five-week-old pup?
>
> Five Weeks to Seven Weeks: Weaning starts; Pup has little sense of fear, participates in litter games; the pecking order begins; the brain takes on its adult sophistication; and, in the seventh week, a human partner becomes the pack leader. Pup is taken home.

Now all of the above has been gleaned from Peter Scott, Clarence Pfaffenberger, Jacob Mosier, Clarice Rutherford, and David H. Neil (the latter two writing in *How to Raise a Puppy You Can Live With*) and from my own observations. Much of it has been verified by the new humane gun dog group: Mike Gould, Gary Ruppel, Ken Osborn, Butch Goodwin, Jim Charlton, and the latest member, Web Parton.

Five other gun dog wizards who are not yet members, but who I counsel with, are Mark Reeves, Ph.D., Knoxville, Tennessee; Reverend Walt Cline, Alliance, Nebraska; John Iacopi, Stockton, California; Dick Royse, D.V.M., Wichita, Kansas; and Jim Culbertson, same town. Reeves is an English setter expert and outdoor writer. Walt is the man who saved

A black Lab pup noses a downed duck on the edge of a stream. Dogs taste with their nose, not their mouth. (Photograph © Bill Buckley/The Green Agency)

the hunting cocker spaniel in America. John is a serious waterfowl hunter, outdoors writer, and connoisseur of Labs. I consider Dr. Royce the top vet in America, and Jim Culbertson is the greatest bird hunter I've ever known.

A Daily Log

I have great fun and receive much value by keeping a daily log of each pup's maturation. I do it with every pup I bring home.

Let's open Cookie's log. It reads:

"Cookie's eight weeks old today, and we got her at five weeks. During these three weeks she has gone from an uncertain and essentially frightened wallflower to a mud wrestler. The dogs ram her, and she rolls and comes up confused but counter attacking. She has a temper.

"Cookie is left-handed and probes with her left paw. She has bonded with me and Molly. I accomplished this by kissing her on the mouth and blowing in her nose every chance I got. Dogs love to recognize and analyze their human partner's breath. I learned this from Bob Wehle. Every time a dog is released from an Elhew kennel run, it races toward a love table: an elevated table Bob has had constructed where the dog gets eye-level with Bob as the man blows in the dog's nose and mouth."

Thomas Fox, Esq.

Thomas Fox, an English country gentlemen and gun dog trainer, writing in *The Complete Sportsman* (1689), tells us he spits in the dog's mouth as a means of bonding.

Tom missed the boat here, because scent is primary to animals in deciphering an individual of any species. It is with scent that the dog bonds. Realize, dogs taste with their nose, not their mouths. All food presented to a dog is first sniffed. If the dog likes it, he gulps it. If not, he'll turn his head from it. Dogs learn to know their human companion best by smelling their breath.

But then, perhaps Tom did make an important point 300 years ago. The dog certainly followed Tom's initiative by passing his own saliva back to Tom; we are all licked by our dogs as a sign of their affection. As explained above, this licking grew out of lapping, where the pup cleaned the mother's mouth after she upchucked the product of her hunt and left morsels about her chin and mouth.

Clock and Calendar Precautions

Now for a final wrap-up on critical periods in a pup's development. All human or canine behavior is variable. Some pups may be precocious and perform feats hardly expected and seldom duplicated by their littermates. There will also be dullards. Plus, different pups will have different motor skills: one's an athlete, the other's a klutz.

So don't put a clock nor a calendar on your pup. Specifically, let your pup have a puppyhood.

I've said before, should you be a plumber, did your parents put a pipe wrench in your crib when you were ten weeks old?

You see how preposterous that would be. By the same token, why attempt to have Pup heeling, sitting, staying, fetching, and running land blinds when he's two months out of the nest?

Well, it has been tried. And in every case it destroyed the pup.

Happy Timing

Instead, let the pup have all the "hunting" games you can think of. Let him fetch tethered pigeons when he's six weeks old. This is not tedium for Pup, it's excitement. And Pup knows when you're pleased. He struts his stuff. Take Pup for walks in fields and woods—especially where there is low cover. Don't want him hit in the face with debris and slowed down or turned back due to rough going.

Let him sniff where the chi-chi bird launched, smell the cow pie, fetch the box turtle, leap back from the splashing dive of a muskrat. Let him learn nature, all aspects of it: cover, terrain, wind, weather, humidity, heat, cold, scents, what have you.

Now you're teaching Pup to be exactly what you want: a gun dog. But you're not yelling, pushing, pulling, or demanding, as you might be in yard training. You can see the difference.

Your voice afield is a gentle, happy voice. This is the voice to bring a positive pup along.

"Why Teach a Dog What He Doesn't Need to Know?"

Professionally I've spent my life as a dog behaviorist, gun dog analyst, and reporter. But some things I wrote thirty years ago are not what I write today. I grew. I mellowed. My ideas expanded and changed. I elevated retriever training to a higher plane. I now know things I never imagined before. And many of you have expanded and changed with me; you know the same things. All of which can be summarized as giving the dog the benefit of the doubt. Letting the dog be the important thing in gun dog training—not the human partner, not some competitive goal, just bird hunting and home living.

Primarily I've learned that formal training is both unnecessary and potentially damaging to the dog. I want dogs up, happy, positive. Training drills, for the most part, are dull, depressing, and faulted with trainer domination.

I do not want dogs hurt, nor do I want them intimidated; it is not necessary to do either.

Class gun dogs are now being developed by letting the dogs have their own head and their own motivation, which means their own gratification. Such dogs are enthused and happy. Such dogs are master hunters, the likes of which we've not see before, and they are good buddies before the fireplace or in the pickup.

Ben Williams

One pioneer in the field of dog motivation and "hands off" training is a quintessential, retired school teacher who is also a master sculptor and oft-published outdoors photographer. His name is Ben Williams, and Ben lives outside Livingston, Montana, where he's in his thirtieth year of breeding and developing what he calls "prairie Brittanies."

You see, Ben hunts parcels of land with venues of 40,000 acres. So he must have a dog with reach and scat to cover this expanse—thus, his long-legged, prairie Brittany.

Ben became one of the most influential mentors in my life with but one hunt. I may not have known it, but I now realize I was prime for what he taught, and he was the man to teach it.

Ben said, "I don't believe in yard training. I just put the newcomer in the pack and let 'em go. The dogs learn by hunting: That's what makes a hunting dog." He then emphasized, "Why teach a dog what he doesn't need to know?"

Ben has other firsts just as vital to our revolutionary gun-dog programming program. He will only train on wild birds, will never conduct a yard drill, cares nothing about the dog learning basic obedience, and essentially instills only one principal command, "Come," with a lesser command being, "Back."

Getting Pup to Come

Delmar Smith once said to me, "The dog's got to come when the come's in you and not the dog." Can you unravel that?

Both Ben and Delmar realize the hardest thing for a dog to do is break off his pleasure and respond to your order to get by his side. The dog's saying, "Why? I'm enjoying this." Gary Ruppel talks a lot about this.

If you can get a dog to come when you call, you can get him to do anything. But consider, as we will later, if the handler yells, "Come here," or blows the suck-in whistle, and the whole pack heads toward him, don't you think the newcomer is going to come along? Sure he is. And that's the best dog training.

And that's relevant to the litter box check cord.

Tying a litter box check cord

Tie knot in end of two-foot cord (upper left hand) and form a loop (lower right hand) part way down.

Insert knotted end through loop—now greater loop, held by pinched right-hand fingers, goes around Pup's neck.

You now have a clinching honda knot that won't slip when you tighten it at the exact size to fit Pup's neck.

The Philosophy and Application of the Litter Box Check Cord

No living thing wants to give up its independence. Therefore, to take the freedom from any living creature can cause a grudge against the disciplinarian.

Consequently, why not let dogs train dogs? Then their gripe is against their own kind and not you.

Makes sense, so here's what we do.

Get some three-eighths-inch nylon cord and cut it in two-foot lengths. Tie an overhand knot in one end (see photos) and place a cord about each pup's neck. Now poke that tied-off end through a clinching honda in the other end of the cord and tighten. Thus you have built a non-slip cord-collar.

Be absolutely sure you've tied a genuine honda. A honda can't slip, so there's no chance of choking Pup. But you must check Pup's growth and loosen the honda if Pup's throat grows too large for the looped check cord.

Now get set to train a pup without breaking his spirit.

One pup in the litter is going to take off ambling sideways. That white check cord, however, is going to slide over another pup's two front paws. The latter pup is going to grab that cord—for all pups are mouth oriented—and when he does he will anchor the traveling pup. He will deny his wandering for the first time. He will put a stop to the moving pup's druthers.

Wow! The traveling pup won't stand for this. Something's got him and won't let go. Besides, who has the right to interfere with his coming and going? This is tyranny. So the roped pup sets up a squall, he leaps and rolls, for he knows death is near.

But then the anchoring pup releases his jaws, and the halted pup goes end over end. Now the victim sets there and dazes about, wondering, "What happened?"

Well, for the first time that pup gave himself over to another living thing's will. And it wasn't pleasant. But what's important, there's no grudge.

And this catch-as-catch-can is repeated throughout the litter. Some pups hold tight. Other pups tug hard on the cord they've grasped in their mouths. The whole litter box is either pulling away or tugging back.

But wait. Two weeks later all you, as a human, have to do is walk over to the litter box, reach down and pick up a cord, and you know what?

Walk a pup away. That's right. The pup will walk on leash. And there's no way you could have taught that pup to do this without a fight and resentment.

And that's dog training: Positioning dogs to self train. Letting other dogs train dogs.

The ideal time to put these cords on a litter of pups is at four weeks. At that time the pups can hear, start to eat food, begin to bark, wag their tail, and, with the first sign of teeth, bite other pups. However, a pup at this age tires easily, which means play won't last long. And that's good.

Vital to our "hold 'em game" is Pup has now started to develop perception; this period also marks the beginning of socialization. Activity picks up with playing, biting, chewing, play-fighting, scruff-holding, prey-killing, head shaking, barking, growling, and snapping. This then is the greatest time of all to put on those check cords.

But note this: The pups start teething at two to three weeks. From three to five weeks they are biting each other with some force. Therefore, from possibly three weeks (four for sure) to five weeks is your best bet for maxi-use of these cords. Because by the fifth or sixth week, each pup's teeth, plus his aggressive disposition, can have the cords completely severed. So that's the end of their usefulness. But in just two weeks they will have conditioned each other for life.

ON OUR WAY

Well, we've started training. The rest of this book sees us leave the litter box and go afield. We'll not be emphasizing yard training but maximum contact with wild game.

We're into motivation here, not domination. We're into training with intimacy, not intimidation. We're going to train with our head, not our hands. And we're going to bring on happy gun dogs with great self-confidence, pleasing personalities, and maximum zest. Joy is our utmost quest.

So I feel you're headed for the gun dog training experience of your life.

5

The Power of Bonding

"The impulse toward rationalism turned humans against
a part of themselves—a part that came to be thought of as base or animal
nature. That part that couldn't be tamed or perfected . . . led to a number of
disorders. Among them a fearful sometimes cruel, and always distorted view of
animals. In that way, the increasing rationalism of the Western mind
led to an increasingly irrational view of animals."
—Joseph Wylder, *Psychic Pets: The Secret Life of Animals*

The goal of this chapter is to prepare you to bring Pup along, to make the dog dream of a lifetime come true before your very eyes. And to know you did it! But you didn't do it the old way.

For it is written in *How to Raise a Puppy You Can Live With* by Clarice Rutherford and David H. Neil: "*If you want a relationship with your dog which is out of the ordinary, then you must do things that are out of the ordinary.*"

Now there are some important thoughts in this book. Neoteny is one. The maximum absorption of stimuli by pups during their first twelve weeks of life is another. And later we'll spend a lot of time familiarizing ourselves with hidden balks and how to overcome them. But now, we may be discussing the most powerfully important single item in this book: how to train Pup.

TRAINING PUP
Well, the best way to train Pup is, *seemingly*, not to train him at all.

Wow, talk about defying tradition. Talk about the muscle pros who'll

Pup will be by your side afield, but she must also be by your side at home. (Photograph © Henry F. Zeman)

swallow their chew on that one. But that's right. You'll remember Ben Williams said, "Why teach a dog what he doesn't need to know?" I now tell you, "Why teach a dog at all?" For it's obvious to me, and it's been proven by me, you don't have to.

Take that human boy or girl in your household. You've taught them the English language, not to potty in the living room, nor to throw their food against the wall. You now know they won't tangle their hair in the home Exercycle, nor break dishes, nor bound into the street. Plus, they know a ton of other stuff.

And how was this taught? In rigid home classroom sessions? In hours of isolation with TV materials, picture books, or a brought-in nanny?

Of course not. These kids were taught to do right as a part of daily living. Never were they actually sat down and run through the verbs *is, am, are, was, were, been, do, did, be,* and on and on.

They learned happily, by osmosis, in a leisurely setting that was pleasant and even cozy.

So that's it! We're going to teach Pup the same way. This old idea of letting Pup out of his crate with all the expectations of the Earps walking toward the O.K. Corral is absurd. We're not preparing for a fight; we're preparing for delight.

FIDO TRAINING

I want to introduce you to FIDO.

FIDO is not a dog. FIDO is this author's training concept. FIDO stands for Filling In and Digging Out the reception and reaction of a dog upon receiving your message. And what's your message? Usually it's a command for Pup to do something.

But you know right off I'm going to reject that approach. Demands are dead because domination in dog training is dead. This is not Marine Corps boot camp. This is your home. Pup's a member of your family the same as Dad, Mom, Son, and Daughter, and Pup's accorded the same thoughtful educational approach as the rest of you.

To repeat, have you drug your spouse into the backyard and locked him or her in a chainlink run holding a doghouse? If you have, how are the two of you bonding?

So I ask you, are you taking your meals with your dog as you do with your spouse? Are you sleeping together? Are you riding in the pickup together? Are you enjoying vacations together? Are you paying any attention to what the other has to say?

If all your answers are "yes," you are building a sure 'nuf gun dog and a friend for life. If they're not, then I request this of you: On each of your hunts don't yell at Pup, don't kick him and throw clods of dirt at him. For you see, Pup's not going to do what you think he should, because you've not been a trainer.

What I'm saying is Pup will never be the pride of your life if you don't let him share your life. And an isolated kennel-run dog is more likely trained the traditional way: commands, dominance, punishment, and disappointment.

Now this kennel damnation I have has nothing to do with the professional kennel where trainers and associates release dogs and work them every day. Those dogs are generally stimulated, prided, encouraged, loved, and appreciated—in the right hands!

TRAINING PUP THE TARRANT WAY

Now everything I write here I've already proven. And if that ain't enough for you, Mike Gould, Ken Osborn, and Gary Ruppel have proven it, too. Then there are recent professional converts such as Butch Goodwin and Jim Charlton and Web Parton that are starting to see the results and like what they see. Others are coming forward.

These pros and I grew together, and we all came to the same conclusion together. Admittedly I'm the most committed to the hands-off approach because I'm not taking in client's dogs. But then, neither are you.

Clients want to see immediate results. They also want absolute control because they usually know little about dogs and have never had a self-directed dog they could trust. Clients can't imagine a dog thinking things out, planning his own hunt, knowing where the birds are at any particular time of day, knowing how to use the wind, understanding the effect of humidity.

Clients feel if a dog gets fifty yards out they'll never get him back. They'll say, "I want a dog that hunts for the gun. That's within gun range. That don't run to hell and gone. I'm not going to put up with any nonsense."

The pro has a mortgage, a pregnant wife, a high-interest loan on his kennel rig, so what's he going to do? He's going to say, "All right." When privately he should be thinking, "Oh God, the same old dead hand of the past. The same old negative approach to gun dog excellence." But money

Your retriever needs to go with you wherever you go. If Pup always stays close, you can train by osmosis. (Photograph © Marilyn "Angel" Wynn)

drives the machine, so the dog is taken in for a highly rigid, repetitive, laborious, dull, and minimally productive training program.

But you, my reader, don't take the dog to a pro. You train him yourself.

You do that by osmosis. Know what that is? *Webster's Dictionary* tells us osmosis is "a subtle or gradual absorption or mingling." For our purposes, it can be defined as an apparently effortless absorption of ideas, feelings, and attitudes.

And that absorption is what Pup does when he lives with you. I mean constantly at your side. And there are several reasons for this. Pup is very bright, intelligent beyond your comprehension. Plus he (or she) is sensitive. So sensitive that Pup has ESP: extrasensory perception. Yes, Pup can read your mind. He can read the smells you transmit, your feelings, your attitudes, your illnesses, your highs, your indifferences, and most important, your eyes.

You tell me, "Bull." Then I tell you back, "How then does a dog realize an epileptic seizure is going to strike his human companion, and force the boy, man, woman, girl, to lie down? How can a dog predict an earthquake? How can a dog demand a camper leave a canyon she wanted to overnight in, only for the woman to discover the next morning the canyon collapsed and all inside were killed?" Still not convinced? The examples are in the thousands.

You'll know Pup's reading you (FIDO—remember, Filling In and Digging Out) because of the expression in his eyes, the set of his ears and tail, the cock or droop of his head, actually so many ways.

Pup knows you, my friend, like he knows his own paw. Yes, that one he's always chewing on.

Now that line above, the one that had the phrase "*seemingly,* not to train him at all." What did that mean? Why was that startling thought put there?

Well, when dogs are in training the traditional way, a witness can see things happen. He can see the trainer jerk the check cord, hear him yell at the dog, see him grow angry and spin around as he throws his fist at the ground. He can see the whites of the dog's eyes, wishing he were anywhere else. He can see the dog's drooped tail.

Give you an example. I was driving down a residential street in my pickup when I saw a teenage girl with a tall dog that probably went 150 pounds. I mean a great, shaggy, leviathan dog.

Trainer Jim Charlton, golden retriever specialist of Portland, Oregon, with one of his prize pupils.

The girl had a leash on the monster, and she was rigid in stance, loud in voice, and furrowed browed. I could hear her through my car door window and the windshield. This gal was yelling, "Heel, sit, stay!" I know that dogs hear much better than we do. But this gal was not only "training" that big dog but also all the dogs in that subdivision. Her voice was that loud, her gestures that menacing.

Understand? Overkill. Overmuscle. Overheavy.

NOW THE WAY WE TRAIN

Pup's been home two days. You're sitting in your easy chair reading the paper. But you catch sight of the rascal ambling toward you so you say, "Come here boy (or girl)." You say it swell, gleefully, happily, cordially, entreatingly.

Pup don't know scat. But he's heard your first command. And I do hate that word *command*. Why not *request*? See what I mean?

Now the pup's at your feet, and he's tired from running so he starts to sit. You've pre-read that in him (Digging Out), you know he's going to sit, so you say, "Sit, Pup"—your second request. This pup is just over five weeks, and he's just received *and performed* two oral requests.

So let's go back to FIDO. You think ahead. You watch Pup. You assume certain things, later you'll know a lot of things. Remember: Filling In and Digging Out. You send messages and receive feedback until both the sender and the receiver share the same concept. And that, my friends, is dog training. And to do that, dog and human must send and receive a ton of messages. And they do. But they must also be on the same medium, using the same channel, and have the same motivation.

Consider: Pup is coming toward you so you fill in (define or compound) his behavior with the request "Come here, Pup." At the same time you also read Pup's feedback. He shows no resentment at your command. He's looking at you with those delightful, baby-blue eyes. He's happy. Your voice is pleasing. You're doing things right. The feedback is positive.

Then you also know Pup is going to sit; he's tired. So the minute he drops his butt you say, "Sit." Once again you have dug out Pup's upcoming behavior. You "read" the dog. His response to himself. And you put a word to it.

In communication theory, all this is called reading body language and feedback. Let me tell you what Clarice Rutherford and David H.

This golden learned to hunt by hunting. (Photograph © Bill Marchel)

Neil, in their book cited earlier, relate. They say that dogs have the power of precognition (telepathy). They say dogs sense our private emotions and read our thoughts. They furthermore reveal that all animals communicate through a silent language. And Rutherford and Neil write that we, too, once had that ability.

They then intimate that beyond our awareness we are constantly sending psychic waves, which dogs can automatically receive. In other words, Rutherford and Neil have witnessed the same phenomena in uncanny communications between dogs and dogs and between dogs and humans, as I have.

So it is counterproductive to attempt to beat or shock a dog to performance when all you have to do is live with him, adjust yourself to his psychic frequency, and watch him blossom. In his book, *Snakefoot: The Making of a Champion,* Bob Wehle writes, "All I speak of here, is done, 'with no kicks or sticks.'"

You're training mentally, not physically. You're enticing, not intimidating. You're paying attention to the dog, instead of demanding he pay attention to you. You're attempting to receive and decipher what the dog's saying more than you're shooting off your own mouth.

I KNOW THE PROBLEM

"That's fine," you say, "but how can it apply to my life. I work all day. I'm gone all day. I can't be FIDOing all the time.

That's America entering the twenty-first century. No longer does man (or woman) work at home; the farmer, the rancher, the blacksmith, the seamstress are going, going, gone.

And in those days when people did work at home, everyone had a trained dog, and no one trained them.

Give you an idea. I recently went up to Boise, Idaho, and gathered a story on seventy-eight-year-old Bill Bennard, a Chesapeake Bay retriever enthusiast.

I was admiring a photo of Bill's dad standing in shallow water on the Missouri River up in South Dakota about 1917 as he put out live English call ducks. (Yep, it was legal in those days.)

The limit on ducks was twenty-five back then, and with a four-man party, this Chesie was retrieving one hundred ducks a day. But, and you've got to get this, nobody had ever trained him.

In the old days, hunters had magnificent gun dogs, and no one trained them. There were no trainers. The dogs learned to hunt by hunting. The dogs were given latitude to develop their own God-given instincts—what we call natural ability. And when two people bred two dogs, they chose sire and dam with pronounced natural ability instead of like today, picking those whose natural faults have been smothered by slick trainers. For pups from the latter dogs will have the parents' faults. Whereas pups from the natural-ability dogs will usually perform just as well as Mom and Dad did. For the ability is bred in, not forced under the hide by some heavy-handed trainer.

The Chesie above was successful with what God put in him, not what man beat into him.

Give you another example.

Momma-Dog

Momma-dog gets pregnant and disappears from the farmhouse. She's gone three months and one day here she comes with eight pups in tow. As time goes by, the farmer learns that those pups know how to hunt, back, and fetch. Those are trained dogs, at three months, and they were taught by watching their mother.

They were taught, folks, by osmosis.

Dogs Training Dogs

With the litter box check cord, we saw how effectively dogs train dogs. You can't beat it. Primarily the pups don't realize what they're doing, they bear no resentment at being led to do whatever comes up, and it's just a blast.

There is no finer way to take a retriever pup to water. Wait until a hot day, walk the pups a long way—have their tongues dragging the trail—then walk them to water, all without saying a word.

They'll crash in. Oh, not all, one will dip a toe, but eventually you'll have the whole litter afloat. And you didn't say a thing. That's dog training.

Or getting the new pup through a dog door. You're on your knees doing it alone. But with a house pack they'll have that new pup out that door in a day.

Happy Timing Again

Also consider this. Nothing, absolutely nothing, does a pup more good

*Nothing, absolutely nothing, does a pup more good than Happy Timing. (Photograph ©
Lon E. Lauber)*

If you bond with Pup early on, you will have a friend for life. (Photograph © Bill Buckley/The Green Agency)

than Happy Timing. That's walking. You out walking with all your dogs. And I repeat, it's the zenith of dog training, nothing else can ever touch it. You'll see the proof in the closing chapters.

And why do pups take to this? They love physical exercise, plus physical contact: bump and run. That's why they're hunting dogs. They'll run to hell and back and love every mile of it, no matter what they must shoulder through. Just as the Iditarod dogs do.

There's so much to Happy Timing. The dogs are competing with each other, leaping each other's back, seeing who can get to the pond first. They learn to honor: One dog gets a scent and they all stop to support him, to learn on their own what he discovered. Nature becomes second nature to them; they learn the hazards of rocks, the mustiness of dead logs, the breathtaking, dusty warmth of a summer wheat field, the tang of persimmons, the stench of a dead opossum, the quickness of a butterfly, the nervousness of a chi-chi bird. They just learn nature. They learn the workplace where they'll ply their trade the rest of their lives.

And where you might have thought pack-running would result in a fight, instead it results in one dog respecting the "territory" of another. That's right: territory. A dog finds game: That's his territory. Another dog bolts in, he's invaded territory. He's not stealing point, as they say, so much as encroaching on private ground. Happy Timing teaches mutual respect.

Happy Timing also builds boldness. Got a shirker? Throw him in the pack. He'll be out front in three days. If not, you better start thinking of giving him to the kid down the road.

The Miracle of Fetching

Clarence Pfaffenberger provides us with one of the most unique and powerful clinical observations. He learned unequivocally that if a pup did not fetch to a person, that pup-grown-to-dog would never make a guide dog. Why? Because that dog did not care to please a human.

I think that's staggering in its importance. The single determinant of whether or not a dog could lead the blind was whether or not he fetched as a pup. Don't you find it staggering, too?

But there's more. Peter Scott used the fetch test for his laboratory dogs and concluded that in training for fetch or in conducting the test for fetch, a pup was never scolded or punished in the attempt. Matter of fact, not scolding and not punishing during the teaching of fetch was found to be more important than during any other teaching exercise.

A Chesie pup shows power stroke while retrieving dummy.

Now she delivers to the hand of her human companion, who gives her a loving touch on the back of her neck.

At the same time, Pfaffenberger decided that guide dog trainers would make, not break, the dogs. Shouting, striking, picking up and flinging, or any other sort of physical punishment was absolutely forbidden. The rule was every dog would be praised for doing good, but none would ever be punished for failing.

Isn't Fetching an Instinct?

And going back to Wehle, the pointer expert. I arranged a conference call for him to speak with several gun dog trainers who were attending a no-pain training workshop at Butch Goodwin's Chesapeake Bay retriever kennels at New Plymouth, Idaho.

One pro, speaking into the phone, mentioned something about a fetching problem. Wehle said, "You have to teach them to fetch? I thought retrievers did that by instinct?"

We make everything so much harder than it needs to be. Think of all the books that teach you how to get Pup to fetch when fetching was the reason he was born.

BONDING

You've heard scientists say that nature abhors a vacuum. Well, so does communication. You can't have two conscious living things in close proximity and not have communication. It's impossible. You may not think anything's transpiring between you and the person sitting next to you in that egg crate arrangement of a commercial jet, but there is—constantly.

And if any two living beings are bonded, the communication is always in some part extrasensory.

Take the old man and his wife of fifty years. She's in the living room reading the paper. He's sitting at the kitchen table. He silently stands. She couldn't have heard him move, but she says, "Where you going?"

He answers, "To the—"

She cuts him off, saying, "Again?"

He replies, "Not for that reason."

"Then what are you—"

He interrupts, saying, "There's a draft."

She says, "Well, it's coming through the—"

He butts in, "No, not the dog door."

And that's the way it goes. They know what the other is going to say before it's said.

Or how often my wife and I—being apart—have dialed each other on the telephone at the same time, having thought of each other at the same moment.

HUNTING

When I was hunting every day and had such an uncanny pack of Labs, it was common to spend a morning such as follows.

We'd enter the field and I'd be thinking, why don't they check that windmill over there? It's got a great stand of sedge about it and though bobwhite don't like the stuff, still it forms an edge with the prairie grass and 90 percent of all birds are found on an edge.

And thinking this I'd see two or three break off and head straight for the windmill. And note I say, "Two or three," for all dogs don't bond to the same degree. Some know you better than you'll ever know yourself, while still others bond with dogs and not people. Or still others just don't have the smarts to think it out.

Then there are men, too, who have the ability to think dog while others do not.

Know How to Think Dog

I've spent a lot of time with Man Rand, who lives on Sedgefields plantation at Alberta, Alabama. Man has many laurels, one being he's the only black man ever elected to the Field Trial Hall of Fame. More important than that, Man scouted nine of the eleven national bird dog championships garnered by the immortal handler, Clyde Morton.

Many now agree that Man's scouting—that is, keeping track of the vying bird dog so it won't get lost, bolt from the course, or take off after nongame—contributed as much to Clyde's nine national wins as the handling ability of the expert himself.

Matter of fact, the present-day owner of Sedgefields, Jimmy Hinton, who still campaigns bird dogs on the national field trail circuit, has told me, "Man Rand just learned to think like a dog. He can ride up top a hill and nine times out of ten look it over and say, 'If I was a dog, I'd go this way.' He's always right."

And that's precisely the way it will be with you and your bonded dog. I cannot emphasize this enough to you. But heed this: Do not adopt an infant pup nor start training until you've read chapter 12 of this book.

Over the Long Haul

A long-haul truck driver called me the other day from far off. He asked if it would work out if he got a dog to ride in the truck cab with him. I told him it would work out perfectly if he did not let the dog out at rest stops on the interstate. They are permeated with filth for a dog.

I hung up and imagined that guy and that dog coming down the 1,000,000th mile of road together. They've not been apart for, what, three years? And that dog and that man know what the other's thinking five miles ahead. "Yes," the dog decides, "I'll have fried onions on my hamburger today." And the truck driver will order fried onions for him without thinking a thing about it.

It is important that the whole family bonds with the dog, though I doubt you'll get much argument on that from any kids in the house. (Photograph © Connie Summers/Behling & Johnson Photography)

DIFFICULT TO DO

I know what I ask you to do seems hard, this requirement you live your life with your dog. For most of us go off to work each day, and the dog stays home. No way can you bond ten, thirty, fifty miles apart.

So maybe I'm writing for twenty or forty years from now—or a hundred years past, huh? When tomorrow everyone has their own workshop in a side room of their house, and everything's done by computer. Even the kids have their school lessons at home. And blue-collar workers—if there are any left—put in three thirteen-hour days and have four days off every week. That'll work. Pup will get to know you with that amount of association.

But you and Pup can bond even with you gone a standard part of five days a week. It just means when you're home you give Pup lots of time. But then, you also have a wife and kids to keep enthused, to let them know you love them. So you have to ration your time, and you have to maximize the quality of all you do with every member of your family—including Pup.

As one woman wrote me, "Oh yes, our Lab is trained, but my kitchen isn't papered, and the back steps are still rickety."

THE FAMILY DOG

Ideally the whole family bonds with the dog. They go to field with you, they walk Pup, they play with him in the backyard.

Several of us trainers went with Jim Charlton, the golden retriever expert in Portland, Oregon, to pick up a stud pup. You know, the pick of the litter. And we all know Mike Gould has an uncanny knack for picking what turns out to be the best of the lot.

So Mike's looking at the pups and talking about kinetic balance (remember up front?), and I'm distracted by a teenage girl who is running the momma-golden through a series of tricks. The old gal is asked to roll over, play dead, beg, sit up, and on and on. And I realized, then, on her own this girl had taken on the responsibility of making that momma-dog a bona fide member of that family. This golden was a hunting dog, but parlor tricks compounded her membership as a special member of that group of humans.

Maybe this is one of few reasons field trials and hunt tests still have value. They surely don't so far as teaching a retriever anything about hunting. But these organized testing days can bring the family to a new locale. There they can socialize with families of identical interest.

I'll never forget running my Labs thirty-five years ago in the field trials at Castle Rock, Colorado. One time a tornado came tearing through. The trial was not stopped. That was uncommon family excitement.

Another time a mother came to a handler who was in the hole blind to run behind me and told him his son was pestering a rattlesnake. The man borrowed a shotgun from one of the official gunners and went to dispatch the dubious pet.

But things could also be normal at trials: picnics, hospitality events at the host motel, budding puppy-love affairs in the motel's penny arcade, and on and on. I remember how each trial ended, one mother yelling out of a car window at another mother, "See you at Cheyenne next week."

Maybe one day somebody will come up with an organized testing arrangement so that retrievers can actually be compared with each other for those things that do happen on a typical day afield. Then both dog and family will benefit equally. I thought I could do that when I created the hunting retriever movement. But it was not to be: Kennel club profits and man's ego turned the test hunts into the old-style field trial format where men—and not dogs—were considered most important.

Once again tests were installed that forced the retriever to trip over his own instincts, and when he couldn't or wouldn't he was too often brutalized into compliance.

THE DOG'S DOOM

And why do I criticize today's retriever field testing? Simple. Man's vanity is the dog's doom. When you and Pup go for a bird, you go as a team: He's the guide and you're the gun. You're pulling for each other. But when man takes his retriever to vie in a test, the man's ego, his penchant for domination, makes it all man and no dog. The retriever becomes a pawn on a chessboard, a serf doing the earthly lord's bidding.

Such men emulate some kind of Paul Bunyan, the ultimate wilderness man, when their actual being is that of a pencil pusher, profit seeker, urban organizer. They get a buzz out of controlling something that is a part of nature: the dog. It feeds their ego, it vents their weak and pathetic urban selves. Urban confinement and restriction and homogeneity prompt some men to seek a primordial bridge to the ancient hunter who was self-sufficient, accomplished without technology, and lived by his wit afield.

It is erroneously felt the only difference between that caveman and this condo dweller is the caveman wore hides and the condo man wears tweed gun club coats, safari boots, silk ascot, capeskin gloves, and an outback hat.

It's the dog that wins their trophies, titles, and hat pins. The dog is to be used, not treated as an equal. It is imperative the man win, for domination is a sickness of man and always has been. Company X raids Company Y. Until one hundred years from now there'll only be one company left that owns the world. Think so?

Nation A invades Nation B. For man is never satisfied; he always wants more. And in the last analysis he will do anything to get it, all at the expense of men and animals and morality. Remember the recent dead bodies in that African river, so thick and deep the human corpses formed a dam? *Domination*.

Unfortunately, it is often the same in retriever training: The old pro works from the hide in. But the humane dog trainer works from the brain out. There's no domination, only inspiration—mentally psyching the dog to do it better than ever before.

The Dog

Me? I think dogs are the best part of us. As the Sacramento pro and flat-coat specialist Ken Osborn says, "The dog is the best deal man ever made." So I fight for them, I protect them, I preach for them. The only reason they are with us is due to their submissiveness. And man uses that very trait against them.

How I wish more wolf had been left in the retriever. When the trainer mistreated him the dog/wolf could go up the trainer's arm like a farm-hand eating an ear of corn.

But no. The retriever suffers and does not fight back.

And therefore, that dog needs my protection and your protection, and the last thing he needs is a field trial to feed some man's ego.

In this book, you'll discover never, never, never do you need to train with pain to have a gun dog that'll hunt with any field champion for a day's outing—and put that champion to shame. God, how lovely that is to do, since we sensitivity trainers have let the dog know he's on his own. The natural retriever knows we're not interfering with his instincts and his natural ability.

Mike Gould calls field trial retrievers "imitation" gun dogs, because they play a game that has nothing to do with hunting, yet are accorded all the publicity and laurels. Like drugstore cowboys.

The field trial and the test hunt retriever is trained to show what man has taught and rigidly controls. The hunting retriever hunts to fulfill what God put in him so he could use his innate skills to catch his daily meals—hijacked now by man taking his find.

Love-Trained Successes

Mike Gould is a specialist at motivating the dog to performance instead of trying to torture him there. His successes are legend. Like Camas, a Lab bitch he whelped. When she was nine months old she was guiding hunters at a big-buck hunting operation and garnering substantial tips for her handlers.

Scarlet, another precocious Lab bitch thrown by the same dad that beget Camas, was fetching big pigeons in a snowstorm at eight weeks of age. She was whistle-trained by Gary Ruppel. Remember Gary, the guy who can't stand for a dog to dislike him?

The hunting retriever hunts to fulfill what God put in him. (Photograph © Gary Kramer)

And Butch Goodwin, the Idaho Chesie specialist. He takes his pups into the bird pen and stands there as the pups deliver the whole lot to him. These pups may be only six weeks old.

None of these guys train with anything but birds, a check cord, their heads, and love. They don't use an electric collar, a cattle prod, a BB-loaded whip, a shotgun shell that'll ever be aimed and fired at a working dog—oh yes, this is common—and no other enforcement device as far as I know. Domination in gun dog training is dead. Love and respect and tons of thinking things out are in.

TRAIN YOURSELF

So the important thing in training a gun dog is first train yourself. A whip-run dog runs based on fear and minimal options. A love-run dog runs based on joy and self-thrust.

So gun dog training is not a matter of force, it's a matter of psychological motivation, of communication. It's not who can yell the loudest; it's who can think the most deeply, develop the most humane and productive techniques, be the best motivator, be the best friend, and be the best communicator—both sending and receiving.

THE MAN WHO IS ANIMAL

So in closing I give you a new word: lycanthropy. It carries a lot of extra baggage in any dictionary. It's all wrapped up with medieval folklore.

Lycanthropy describes a man who thinks he's become an animal. But dictionaries will tell you the man is a werewolf, the result of mental illness or magic.

Well, let's look at lycanthropy today. Is that not what prehistoric man had and lost? Is that what some of us are finding access to in our sensory packet today? Has there ever been a successful hunter who couldn't read animals? And is to read the animal not to become that animal?

I say if you don't know how a particular animal or bird thinks, you can't dupe that animal or bird to your gun. It's that simple. You must know the decoy, the hide, the migration routes, the favorite habitats, the flying characteristics, the eating habits, and so many other things about ducks to get a duck.

Well, we were all turned away from thinking lycanthropy during those centuries animals were considered base and man sublime, when slaughter was encouraged. And the worst of slurs was to say, "He's just an animal."

I now know to grant a dog exceptional psychic powers is to admit to my own and your own. Yet science denies intuition. Didn't Darwin kill God for those without faith? Faith alone just wasn't enough for some when all those ancient bones were excavated. Science prevailed. Except for us with faith. And faith has always served me better than science. Maybe it has for you, too.

So when I say the sensitive trainer has become dog, it's because he can think dog.

Tomorrow's training will not depend on how well the dog accommodates himself to the human but rather how well the human can decipher the dog with the utmost sensitivity, thereby realizing performance never attained before by having tapped the dog's mind.

CONCLUSION

Well, that's it: two ways to train Pup.

Me, I'll opt for osmosis, for FIDO.

But you?

You may not feel you have that kind of time.

So you go for the nylon collar and the rope, for a small amount of manhandling. Well, take along this caution. Don't ever be the heavy. Keep your voice pleasant or neutral. Your eyes betray your inner thoughts. Pup is always reading them. Keep them under control.

For you can lose Pup with heel, sit, stay, and come. And to go one step further: One maniacal act can destroy Pup forever.

If you have the time for osmosis (FIDO), you'll be far ahead, since you'll never be viewed by Pup as negative nor oppressive. Pup will see all training as play, or he won't see it at all.

Remember, sensitivity is in, insanity is out. Read the dog to performance, don't try to muscle him there. Train with your head, not your hand. And be not only Pup's trainer but also his best friend.

6

Yard Training Little,
Field Training Lots

*"One hot, smoky, dust-ladened night a bunch of Marines were fighting
a mountain grass fire at Camp Pendleton, California. Through all the smoke
and sweat and tumbledown rocks a Southern voice was heard to say, 'Let the
damned thing burn . . . it ain't gonna cross the Mississippi anyway.'"*
—Author

Some things some people think important don't matter a hill of beans
to others. That's the way with yard training.

So you may not gather the significance when I say, "Never train Pup
with rigidity and muscle and exasperation. There's too great a chance
Pup may view you as the heavy, your voice is too loud, your actions too
quick, your facial expression too aggravated."

USING HIS OWN HEAD

My ideal for training a pup is to let him go. Let him hit the hills and top
the crests and learn what's on the other side. Let him feel the wind, and
swim the creek, and find his way through the alfalfa. Let him learn the
snow and ice and hail and sun so hot it makes the earth scorch his pads.
Let him do all those things out in nature that were done by the pregnant
farm bitch who whelped in the field and brought her pups in three
months later, totally trained to hunt.

This is so important because Pup will work his life afield. Oh, I
know only two months or so are open season. But hunting for Pup is
Valhalla; nothing can match it. Nothing.

A ten-week-old Chesie explores a duck boat. (Photograph © Lon E. Lauber)

Lying in front of the fireplace is cozy, but breaking ice to get a duck is Pup's crazed mission in life.

When Pup Jumps the Track

Plus, there is always this caution. *When Pup jumps the track (and he will) it is only through discipline you can get him back on line.* It's imperative you remember this. In other words, the day will come when Pup's too busy to come, or too hung up on something to sit straight at heel, or too antsy to even sit. You know?

Well, that can best be corrected by taking time out, getting Pup out of the bird field—quite away from the bird field—and running him through his ABC's. When the session's over and Pup's settled—like the good ol' boys say, "When you got a handle on him"—then hype him up with clapped hands and happy voice and return him to the bird field once again. This is a case where discipline re-claims a dog.

What most people want is to get a handle on Pup. And this is restrictive, this is denying Pup his druthers.

So easy goes it.

Yard Training

Yard training has nothing to do with a bird. Never. For never can anything go wrong between you and Pup where there's a bird involved.

Pup was sent here to be a feather merchant, his whole life is dedicated to birds, and we can never let a bird be part of a bad experience. We can never lessen that zaniness Pup has for a bird one bit.

So what we're going to teach in the yard is heel, sit, stay, and come.

Heel

Proper heel is for Pup to be at your left side (the non-gun side for most people) with his body squared away to the exact front, his near shoulder next to the seam of your jeans, and his head far enough out front that he can see 180 degrees.

The way to come to heel is to have Pup on leash and be walking him in a straight line. Gradually milk Pup—gathering the leash in hand—to your side as you proceed until you have Pup in position. Now stop.

Pup will be surprised at first and may fight you. Keep quiet, or if you say anything, let it be in a whisper. Be calm and pleasant (remember Pup can sense your mood) and wait for Pup to settle. He's full of vinegar, so take your time.

WHY HEEL?

Now why is Pup heeled?

First off, that would be the position in a dove field or sometimes at a duck blind—surely at a green timber shoot. Heeling steadies Pup, keeps him manageable.

Also, heeling cocks Pup for casting. Say you want to send him for a mark: You shot a bobwhite and it's down twenty feet to front and a little to the right side.

Well, move your body. Get straight with that bird. I said it was cocked. Don't ever cast Pup when he's not on line with the objective. Never.

So you shuffle your feet, or you take your right hand and hold it over Pup's head, and snapping your fingers, you tell him to heel as you move your hand about in front of you until it goes behind your right side. Eventually Pup will follow the snapping fingers.

Now when Pup crosses your body and goes behind you to return to your left side, you've adjusted 95 degrees to the bird so Pup's heeling in a straight line toward the downed quail. And how did you adjust?

Two ways. One, you mark something prominent close to the downed quail. A stand of blazing sumac, for example. Or, and I do this all the time, you slice the side of your boot sole in a straight line between you and the bird. Pup will be heeled with this gouged-out line facing directly toward the bird.

That's called re-heeling. And you always do it. If you cast Pup off toward a mark and he's off-center at the line, he'll go the way he's facing, which will be in error.

There's other reasons, besides game, that you heel Pup. You're approaching a sludge pit. You don't want Pup in that gunk, so you heel him and walk past. Or there's an interstate. You can't afford to have Pup bolt and get hit by a car. Heel him to you. And so it goes. A mad bull in the next pasture, a tainted pond or one with glass and jagged metal in it, any hazard you want Pup to avoid, you heel.

Also you heel Pup to inspect him. He leaped sideways just a moment ago. God forbid he came across a rattlesnake. Or did he cut himself when he went through that barbwire fence? Got a cactus spine in a pad? You heard yelping—he didn't come across a coyote in that deep brush, did he?

You also heel Pup prior to kenneling in your home, your car, the motel room. Heel is a preparatory position for Pup to do a lot of things.

SIT

Keeping Pup close and faced in the right direction, lift the leash with your right hand—Pup's to your left—which will raise Pup's upper torso by his neck collar.

Make a spread of your fingers and place the thumb and little finger just above and ahead of Pup's hips—there's a recess there—and press down with your left hand. Pull with the right and press with the left until Pup finally collapses.

And when he does heel or sit, get heavy with the praise. "Why Pup, you're the greatest dog who ever lived. You know what you just did? Oh, my little boy, you just learned your first lesson. And you did it so great." By this time Pup knows he's the carnival candy box that has the gift in it.

Run through the drill again or forget it. With heavy-duty training like this, five minutes may well be enough. Pup has a very short attention span. You don't train him with sustained time, you train him with a repetition of short concentration and then release.

RUPPEL AGAIN

And don't forget Gary Ruppel and his whistle. Gary is an acknowledged master pro who feels the whistle doesn't carry the emotion that can be betrayed by a handler's voice.

Let me take a minute and show how Gary works. Yesterday a man brought a Weimaraner to him, nine months old, drilled to tedium with meaningless backyard heel, sit, stay. Gary told the man what was wrong with the dog. And then you know Gary. There he is with that happy whistle and big grin and telling the dog he wants to be friends.

Well, in forty-five minutes, the condo-dead Weimaraner fetched a duck from the pond, pointed two planted pigeons, ran around the perimeter of the place, came seventy-five yards on a come-in whistle, kissed Gary about ten times, and even showed a friendly paw to the man who brought him. The dog did not want to go home.

Gary told me, "For that guy it was like he'd gone out through this field a thousand times to get the cows. Then one day he saw something shine in the earth. So the next night he brought a shovel. And he dug up gold. That treasure was there all the time, but the man never caught the

Dogs given maximum confidence will pay you back with thrills such as space-walk water entries. (Photograph © Kent and Donna Dannen)

Labs walk at heel on the left-hand side (opposite the gun of most hunters), with the trailing check cord over handler's opposite shoulder.

A handler commands heel and stops walking: the dog stops. The handler says, "Sit," as he pulls up on check cord with right hand, and presses down Pup's hips with left hand. The dog can't help but sit.

Handler tells Pup to "stay" both verbally and with traffic cop's hand signal.

The handler tosses check cord to front . . .

. . . then backs away, holding cord, and repeating both the verbal command to "stay," as well as showing hand signal.

At the cord's end, the handler waits to make sure Pup continues sitting, then gives the command, "Here," or "Come," and quickly milks in cord as Pup approaches. When Pup arrives, the handler commands, "Heel," and the drill starts over again.

gleam of it from the right perspective. This is what must happen to all dog owners."

STAY

You'll realize we teach sit while we are heeling. Your command sequence is heel, sit, stay. Stay is the anchor command. The heel command gets Pup to your side, but sit and stay nails him to ground.

The stay command is imperative when doctoring Pup. He'll want to fidget and exit. Sit-and-stay will hold him. So it must be ingrained. This is where you tell Pup, "Sit, stay," then you walk off, go around the corner of the house, peek back, make sure that rascal doesn't move. Stand there, tempt him, but return before he relaxes and starts to leave.

Sit-and-stay is also the perfect way to keep Pup from greeting strangers or friends by jumping on them. He can't jump if he's sitting.

The sit-and-stay command will also anchor Pup in the back of your Jeep before opening the tailgate. Too often a dog has bolted when that door cracked ajar. And the dog has been killed.

STAY IS SITTING HARD
More about stay.

The best way to teach stay is to have Pup heeled with your check cord in hand, then walk forward, turn around, and face Pup.

But wait a minute. Let's have an equipment check.

THE CHECK CORD
A check cord is woven nylon, two-thirds of an inch thick, let's say, and soaked in a mud puddle about three days then dried in the sun to give it backbone. Otherwise you'll be working with a long noodle that's impossible to control. And we're going to control this check cord as skillfully as any cowboy handles a lariat.

This check cord is attached by a swivel snap to a nylon collar, wide and heavy-duty, with an industrial strength D-ring. Don't shirk on price here, get the best of both. For you know this is essentially all the money you'll ever have to spend for training equipment. That's right, I can teach you to train any breed of gun dog with no more than a cord and collar.

Magazine ads say you've got to have an electric shock collar. This instrument of brutality costs hundreds of dollars. Spend that money to paper your wife's kitchen, then she'll let you back in the house and won't be complaining about you to me.

One more thing.

THE BOWLINE KNOT
When you tie that check cord to your swivel snap I want you to use a bowline knot. I'll show you how to tie it, then I'll explain why it's important.

A bowline knot is tied some six inches from the collar's D-ring. Precise distance is determined by measuring the length of your dog's nose from his collar.

Why is that? Well, a bowline knot is a knot. It's also tied at the very end of a check cord that you can handle with maximum accuracy. And you can do that because you practice just that.

In the old days the philosophy of dog training was repetition, association, and point of contact. In other words, all lessons are repeated, a point of contact is used to maintain control of the dog, and association transfers the need for contact and repetition to only your voice. Your voice will be your total control.

Well, the humane trainers have changed most of that. We'll study the new methods in subsequent chapters.

POINT OF CONTACT

Anyway, the check cord is our point of contact. And the bowline knot is our implement of authority. In the old days, it was roughly used; now we're as gentle with it as a mother's kiss.

We especially use it to break hidden balks; remember, in the prologue I promised we'd learn all about them. They, along with neoteny and our novel use of the critical periods in a puppy's life, are the major contributions in this training book.

Okay, here's what we do.

Get a tape measure and place the end against Pup's collar at the center, bottom of his throat. Extend the tape to the tip of Pup's nose. That's how far from Pup's collar the bowline knot will be tied. However, the check cord is attached to the D–ring via a swivel snap, and this hardware may be an inch long or so. That inch has to be included in the measurement.

A bowline knot is one that will not slip nor tighten. It is given to us by the tall ship sailors of yore. Where you get most of your length from the collar to the nose is in the big loop that attaches to the snap swivel. Follow instructions as I have photographed them, and you'll have no problems.

Now in the old days when we wrote about the bowline knot we'd call it the enforcement knuckle. No more. You don't slap that knot into Pup's jaw. You actually get to the place where just to hint you're going to snap your wrist and the dog will shape up. So never strike Pup with the bowline—just tap him.

The principle is you're standing to front, Pup has turned you off during a training session, you want his attention, so you snap your wrist, which starts a wave down the check cord, and that propels the knot into Pup's lower jaw. This in turn lifts Pup's head up so he's looking at you. For you can't train a dog if you don't have eye contact.

You get good with the knot by having a buddy connect the snap swivel to a cord tied about his wrist. When activated the knot strikes your helper on his bare palm or fingers. You stand distant and give your verbal

Tying the Bowline Knot

Thread the rope through the ring on the swivel snap. Make a loop in the rope approximately six inches from the end of the swivel snap. The precise distance is determined by measuring from the tip of your dog's nose to his collar.

Thread the end of the rope through the loop, from underneath.

String the end of the rope back through the loop created between the swivel snap and the evolving knot, also starting from underneath the loop.

order just as the snap swivel taps your buddy's flesh. As you propel the cord to tap with the knot, your word of command—whatever that is— must come just as the knot touches Pup's jaw. The helper can tell you if you're in sync. And you must know this: Timing is everything in handling points of contact in gun dog training.

We'll want this bowline knot when we get to breaking up hidden balks. You'll see!

BEFORE OUR EQUIPMENT CHECK

We were moving along, teaching sit, when I suddenly jumped track and said, "Let's have an equipment check." Then we examined the check cord and the bowline knot.

Well, back to sit or to sit hard (stay).

String the end of the rope back through the original loop, this time over the top, as shown.

Pull tight while maintaining your bowline knot at the proper distance. Snip off the excess rope.

Bowline knot: properly tied and exactly spaced from collar to tip of your Lab pup's nose.

You've told Pup "Sit" or "Stay." Now you walk away from him, carrying your check cord in hand. Constantly you glance back, monitoring Pup. Should he start to move, say sternly, "Sit," "Stay," or "Hey," or whatever you want as you roll your bowline knot.

Now you face Pup with check cord at the ready. Should he break and move toward you, you've already missed it. For you weren't pre-reading your dog.

Before Pup can stand to break, his shoulder muscles must quiver. Be watching. The moment you see that faint shoulder movement, roll that check cord to bump Pup under his chin with the bowline knot, just as you simultaneously say, "Stay." Or blow one long toot on your training whistle.

So what happens then? Well, anytime you raise his head you tuck in his butt. So up comes Pup's head to avoid the bowline, and in and down goes his butt. To what end? To sit. So one bump and Pup is sitting again. That's dog training. No hassle, no heavy hand, just appropriate equipment and instant timing.

Now the task is to get Pup to come to you. You've just nailed him to the ground hard: now can you move him? Say "Come." Nothing? Say it again.

This time say, "Come," as you give the cord a tug. Oh ho, he's moving. You've got it made. You can nail him or move him, and that's the hardest part of stationary training. A word about handling that cord on come: Guide the cord in one hand and milk with the other. That's proven to be the fastest way.

TEACHING WITHOUT A CHECK CORD

Now nothing is as hard to teach a human or an animal as come without a point of contact. Nothing.

Come means for the person, or dog, to give up what they've found pleasurable and come to you for seemingly nothing. That amounts to a bum deal.

And what's really difficult about all this is that the come has to be transferred orally from you to the dog. And unlike using the bowline knot, *you now have no check cord attached to Pup*, so you must move him mentally.

Invariably amateur trainers do the absolute wrong thing. They end up chasing the dog, hurling epithets of doom. Who, I ask you, can outrun a retriever?

Or they entreat the dog to come to them, get him near, and then whomp him good. That's bright. Now the dog knows he should never come, for if he does he's going to get pummeled. What else can you think of to do wrong?

Well, you know how we teach come? We started in the house. Anytime that coming was Pup's idea we put a friendly word with it: "Come." We also used it displaying Pup's favorite toy. And we called him with, "Come here Pup," each time we fed or walked out back.

So Pup knows what we're saying. But still, that dead sparrow he found is mighty savory. Why should he run off and leave it since he's found out in the past if you see him eating trash you're going to disassemble?

A first-class retriever can be trained through daily conversation and daily living. There's no need to beat it into him. (Photograph © Gary Kramer)

Well, this is Armageddon. Make it or break it.

INDUCING COME

There are several things you can do. Get down on your knees. When you're reduced in size, you appear less formidable and dogs are inclined to run to you.

Or you can start walking the other way. Dogs can't stand to be left behind. They'll usually run to catch up with you. We use this trick all the time to get Pup to fetch the dummy he's standing out there holding.

And if walking away won't do it, running away will. Few dogs can resist chasing a runaway man. And you need not move when running; you can run in place.

But you can never pursue Pup, you can never get heavy-handed with Pup, and you can never lose your temper. This is extremely important. The most important thing in your relationship. If you have a dog that won't come to you, then you have no dog at all.

Another way to approach all this is to outfit Pup with a twenty-foot check cord. Mosey about and see if you can get to the end of the thing. Walking past or at a tangent to Pup won't spook him. Never look at him. Dogs are especially eye conscious. Then when you've got the cord you say, "Come" and gently milk Pup in. Don't horse him. Do so and you've blown it all. Now you've got a fighting fish out there, and he says you're not going to land him.

So take it easy and take your time. Be soothing in your voice. Stoop or kneel down. When Pup gets to you, love him. Don't punish him nor correct him. Love him.

Now keeping the check cord in hand slowly walk off, all the time pepping Pup up, and finally when you get to the end of the cord say, "Come on, Pup," and see if he won't follow you. If so, you're a dog trainer who just won a victory.

Well, that's about it.

From now on we'll be working afield.

Anxious?

I am too. Let's get going.

But one thing—before we turn the page I want you to remember all we taught in this chapter could have been learned by Pup through osmosis: FIDO.

The Natural Way To Train

Just through daily conversation and daily living all of this would have become second nature to Pup. Not with those particular words of command, maybe. Like I'm walking with a load and see there's a pack of dogs laying in my path. I say, "Scoot." That's just normal for me. And the dogs part like the Red Sea.

Or they're digging a hole in the yard and I yell out, "Hey there," which is what I'd yell at a trespasser back there. The dogs come running.

As I was writing the last sentence the dogs alarmed at the front door. I let them vent as long as I could then said, "That's enough." They fell silent as a tomb.

"Let's go" means a car ride. "Get your ball" means find your ball so we can play fetch. "Want your bone?" means it's time for a treat.

Just in our daily interaction and my comments along the way words become part of Pup's vocabulary. "Stay," I say, going out the door to the garage, for every dog wants a car ride. They all know stay. You should see their pouty faces.

It's not my purpose to teach language, but every dog on the place knows more than one hundred words, and many know two hundred plus. And what's important about all this? You can teach the same thing.

And so it goes. Dogs become human through constant association and know everything you're saying to them. The delight and value of it all is that there's no formal training session, no commands, no status differential where I'm in charge and they better do my bidding. Matter of fact, if asked, each of those house dogs would say they're running things.

And I want them to feel that way.

They're my kids.

7

Birds

"Now, let's see how far we are with Mr. Snakefoot.
He has been walked more than one hundred times [Happy Timed],
is only eleven months old and is now ready to be sent to Gary and Diane [pro
trainers] for his final development before being campaigned. He has probably
pointed or flushed seven or eight hundred liberated quail. He has learned to tell
pretty well if there is a bird in front of him or if it has left. He has learned
to back his litter mates on sight."
—Bob Wehle, *Snakefoot: The Making of a Champion*

The retriever pup—just as Snakefoot—must spend his youth in pursuit of birds that he will maul, drag, lick, bite, and fetch.

So you must learn how to handle birds: in hand, in transport, in planting, in hunting, in fetching. Any liberated or wild game bird will do (except pheasant). Most trainers prefer pigeons since they are hearty, transport well, plant well, have a strong odor, and even fly home without your bothering to gather them up or tote them.

About those pheasants. They are vicious birds, rough outs, alley fighters, equipped with a dagger of a beak, and spurs on their legs that can kill. We send no baby retriever for one, dead or alive, until the pup has grown in the bulk and skill to handle them.

BOBWHITE
Of all the birds available to us I prefer bobwhite. They have scat, thunder, the penchant to relocate for successive contact, and a mesmerizing scent. Try to shy away from liberated quail. Why? Because sporting dogs some-

A black Labrador retriever holds a pintail drake. (Photograph © Bill Marchel)

Bobwhite: the ultimate training bird.

times work liberated bobwhite too close, then, when put on their wild cousins, they bump their find.

Bird dogs (and that's what your retriever pup is) can be trained on most any game bird. I recall the guinea was brought to this country for the sole and express purpose of training bird dogs. And Mike Gould has written his name atop the innovator list by climbing 10,000 feet and training his string on Rocky Mountain blue grouse.

BLUE GROUSE

Mike's method is to cast a seasoned gun dog to field, and let him locate and voluntarily stand. Then Mike check cords his pack of pointer and Lab pups into the grouse's scent cone, waits for the dogs to point (pointers) or whoa (retrievers), then releases the all-age dog to flush. Don't think that won't put an edge on the kindergarten set.

CANADIAN TRAINING

And big-time bird dog pros take their strings to Canada each summer to work on Hungarian partridge and sharptail grouse. Upon return to Dixie,

these dogs transfer to bobwhite in a heartbeat.

WORKING PUP WITH A CHECK CORD

In the beginning, you always work Pup with a twenty-foot trailing check cord. Now you've got some way to catch him. Plus, you can adjust his position about the bird without too much fuss by adroitly handling the cord.

Remember the bowline knot—Pup's whoaed on birds. You walk in a great circle about him with check cord in hand. You're continually saying, "Whoa," while you read Pup's shoulders. If there's a tremor there, Pup's about to break, so you flip the cord and send the bowline knot into Pup's chin. This startles him, he forgets what he was going to do, and he once again stands at whoa.

And why walk in a great circle? Walk too close to Pup and it incites him to break. You're moving forward, so why can't he?

HARDMOUTH

If you have a pup that wants to chew the carcass of a dead bird or actually

No longer a pup, this yellow Lab was kept busy fetching pheasant for two hunters.

bites down on a live one, then work that prospect only on frozen birds. Hardmouth must be "nipped in the bud," as Barney Fife used to say.

In the beginning, you couldn't care less how Pup brings the bird to your feet. He may be so small he drags it with a wing tip. It's learning how to handle birds that's important, not the style in which it's done. And notice I said "to your feet." Bringing to hand can wait. However, we know you'll be crouched down to take the bird, if you can.

And when tossing a bird out for a baby retriever to fetch, do it only in short grass. Lessen all hindrances. Have nothing confront Pup to slow him down or put him off game.

A RUNAWAY DOG

And when Pup grabs the bird and takes off, don't chase. Get down low and encourage him to come to you. Doesn't work? Then walk the other way, hollering, entreating. No deal? Then play like you're running away, but you're actually standing in place, marking time. Reach down and grab Pup (or the bird) when he goes by.

If Pup drops the bird afield and wants to leave it, go out there, chatting encouragement, then lift the bird up by your toe and send it flying a few feet. Pup's interest will be rekindled, and he'll pounce on it.

At no time is Pup ever reprimanded for anything that happens with a bird. Everything is positive, upbeat. All he does is successful.

THE ULTIMATE BIRD

Let's say it's 1920 and you're hunting the bird basket of the world: Kansas. There are thousands of bobwhite and the dog—be it pointing dog, retriever, or spaniel—finds a covey and busts it up, then takes off chasing. Hundreds of birds later the dog has learned he can't catch them so he stands and watches them depart. Scads of birds later and the dog starts honoring the birds' scent cone and slamming to point or to a flusher's whoa.

There's been no force-breaking, no heavy hand, no shouting, stomping, flinging your arms around. Nothing. Constant bird contact has built you a bird dog.

So it's not 1920, and you're somewhere besides Kansas and bobwhite are as scarce as lottery winners. We can still do several things. Buy several pen-raised quail and go to a farmer to ask if you can seed them in his field. Tell him you'll pay him to earn this privilege, or you can offer to do a little work for the privilege.

Or you can join a gun dog club or shooting preserve that's interested only in hunting—not politics, skylarking, or shootin' the bull. If the club doesn't have birds seeded, then you buy some and put them out. And here's the way to do it.

JOHNNY HOUSE

Get permission from management to build yourself a Johnny house for bobwhite. Johnny houses don't go for *Good Housekeeping* awards. They're made of wood and fine-net screening so birds don't insert a wing tip and break it off.

Professional Buddy Smith of Collierville, Tennessee, uses an old cotton wagon. Bob Wehle of Midway, Alabama, has built wood structures on stilts with judicious screening, leaving wood areas to block prevailing winds. You can use most anything.

The principle of the Johnny house is to house birds so they can rest and feed, receive water, and be free of predation. Then when you go to the house, you open a flap of your own construction, shoo the birds to flight, let them settle, and begin training.

Most released birds return to enter a funnel of screen (small port inside) placed four inches above a platform from which they fly to a roost. Now they're trapped until your next training session.

It's imperative that one quail (male or female) be left in the structure as your callback bird. This bird will reassemble most of them before sundown. By then your birds are back, you've had a "hunting" training session, and your dog has been into birds.

BIRD FEEDERS

There are other ways to introduce Pup to birds. Put out feeders to attract quail and supplement with feed plots. These sources of grain will become targets of opportunity for both your liberated birds and wild birds to feed. Plus, your dogs will quickly learn this is where they make bird contact. Birds will reassemble about the feeder when you're gone. But so will snakes, opossums, mink, and all other sorts of carnivores.

Because of this, the late John Olin of Winchester fame had his wildlife biologist, bird-wizard Francis Frazier install flash cameras on feed plots so he could determine his primary predator. What was it? The opossum. Today, most hunters figure it's the government-protected hawks.

Pigeon loft above stables.

Others say coyotes.

John had great wealth and could do many things you and I couldn't manage. He'd have large trucks filled with corn drive the interior roads and spread kernels through aft-mounted spreaders as another source of bird feed.

Delmar Smith, the junkyard dog trainer of Edmond, Oklahoma, (and trainer of Brittanies who won ten national championships) would scrounge all of his feeder materials from some dump. He'd take a rusted-out, five-gallon can or bucket, nail the can to a tree trunk, install a callback bird, keep water and feed in the can to sustain it, and replace the bird within two weeks so it wouldn't go stir crazy. Delmar would then spread feed for the covey about the ground.

Sure, the rain will mildew it, and the cattle will stomp it into the ground, and all the varmints in ten counties will come to eat the birds that eat the grain. Plus, you'll meet some mighty big bull snakes in certain parts of the country. But at least you're trying to get training birds, and perseverance will prevail.

PIGEONS

Now there's an entirely different way of going about this bird business. Build a pigeon coop and buy some homing pigeons. But don't let them loose, or they'll fly back to the person from whence they were purchased. But release their beget. For they'll be your training birds and home to your place.

Now get a transport pen, take Pup and your pigeons—which will be hobbled—to the bird field. Throw a tarp over the car windows so Pup can't see you plant the birds. Return to your car and release Pup to train. You'll have a full training session over live birds, seldom lose one (unless it's necessary to shoot one for a particular gun dog problem), and your dog will be bird trained. Not yard trained. Not drilled incessantly with no bird so the poor dog really has no idea of your eventual intent. He will know a birdless outing is unnatural and boring.

TRANSPORTING BOBWHITE

You can also transport bobwhite to the field. Get yourself a portable callback pen. They're available from every gun dog supply store. Go to field. Once again, keep Pup from seeing you plant the birds, park your car in a the shade, put your callback pen at the spot of release—*with the callback bird in it*—and start Pup hunting.

A couple hours before leaving the training field, stow Pup in the car, then read a book or fish in a nearby pond, and your callback bird will sing its head off as most if not all of your training birds reassemble naturally, since that is their custom at dusk.

Drive home and store your birds in your backyard bird pen.

So you see, there's just no reason for not training over live birds. Even if it's thirty miles out of the city to birdland. You can at least manage that drive once or twice a week. And time spent with Pup over birds is maxi-time.

Here's the proof. The worst of the non-bird trainers are the retriever specialists. They hope a dummy can answer their need as a non-bird. Well, it won't.

Bird dog people just pass up any training session that doesn't have a bird, unless it's dangling a bird wing from a fishing rod for a fresh pup.

And flushing people use birds even in their yard drills. They are the ultimate bird users of all gun-dog trainers. Plus, they need a third bird species to get the total job done, and that's the pheasant.

Of course, the other birds we'll hunt with Pup are the duck and the goose. For this we train by hunting. See chapter 8.

LEASING PIGEONS

Now there are other ways to get this bird thing accomplished. You can lease pigeons from a homing fancier. Say you take out five pigeons a session at so much per bird. When finished training let those pigeons loose, and they'll fly home. That way you don't have to tend to them nor build a structure. If a bird dies, you have a set price you pay for the pigeon fancier's loss.

GUNS

Guns naturally go with birds. You've been preparing for this day all along by going distant when Pup is eating and firing a blank .22 pistol. Pup never even looks up. Great!

Or you've been firing that same pistol when Pup, or Pup and the household pack, has been Happy Timing afield. "Bang" goes the .22. This time you were a little close. Pup stops and spins around, looking.

Don't acknowledge him. Look the other way, walk the other way, reach down and pick up a stick; you had nothing to do with the sound that turned Pup about. When Pup shakes it all off, follow along, extend your distance, and when the whole pack is doing something that has their undivided attention, fire the pistol again.

Do this day after day until Pup pays you no mind. Now you're train-ing a gun dog without causing gun-shyness. And notice: both feed time and Happy Time are pleasure times for Pup. The gun is always associated with pleasure.

Now I say gun. Yet I was training above with a blank pistol. Many pros reject the pistol. They say the sound is too sharp, it hurts Pup's ears, or it cuts through where a "boom" sound would come more muffled.

I admired the late Al Brenneman of Frankewing, Tennessee. He was an old-time pro who excelled in curing gun-shyness. He always told me to get rid of the pistol. I can see him now, his tall, craggy frame, following a brace of pups (among bird dog pros a pup is usually nine months or older) down a shelter belt, working them on live birds.

He'd carry a single-barrel, single-shot piece painted Day-Glo orange so he could find it after he'd tossed it in the brush to go correct a dog. I know the gun well for I've seen Al train with it, plus I was standing in his

The handler places a pigeon in the trampoline bird launcher, then backs away, pulls the cord, and the pigeon is catapulted to air.

bedroom that night he handed it over to Wilson Dunn of Grand Junction, Tennessee, to place in the Field Trial Hall of Fame.

Al was taught by Er Shelley of Columbus, Mississippi, possibly the greatest gun dog trainer of all time. At least Er is the only trainer I know of who trained up a pack of coonhounds for multimillionaire Paul Rainey (called "Poor Paul," because his dad cut him off at $40 million), so the man could hunt lion in Africa like he'd hunted rabbits in Mississippi. Rainey stayed at it eight years. It must have been an obsessive sport.

Well anyway, I say use the pistol discreetly. For a pup to us is around five weeks old—not nine months. That pistol fired at a distance is not a shock to a pup. And later, I want you to forego the .410. I find they pattern poor and carry little shot, and what you shoot I want to fall. There's only one gun and that's the .12 gauge, single-shot preferred. A multishell gun is far too dangerous for training dogs afield.

A junk gun is what you need for training, since nothing is as important as the pup. Your attention is always on him. The gun may be cast aside (in dog training you're sometimes required to move fast), dropped in the mud, left in the rain, forgotten in the middle of a gravel road, whatever. Just don't have anything so fancy you hesitate using it.

Like Delmar Smith, once said, "Get a new saddle . . . toss it in the water trough. A new pickup? Run it through a briar patch. Now you don't have to worry about messin' either of 'em up."

As close as you'll be working birds, $7°$ shot will bring the biggest and toughest of 'em down.

OTHER EQUIPMENT

You know I am anti-technology. I couldn't care less what's on Mars. There's no birds there. But there's one device that can help you train Pup, especially if you have no one to be a bird boy.

I'm thinking of a bird launcher. That's a trampoline device in which you place a bird, then by hand-pulled cord or electronic remote, you cast the bird into the air. You can use this instrument so many different ways.

But launchers are expensive and where you could use three, let's say, you may only be able to afford one. I say three for that's the number you'd need to cast multiple marks.

Remember, a mark is a bird that appears afield, is shot, and falls to ground. Pup sees it during its entire flight.

A blind, on the other hand, is a bird planted afield out of sight of the dog, and the dog is cast to find it with the handler directing him with a whistle-and-hand signal.

There are all kinds of variation of the two. For example, a bird boy afield might toss a bird in a great arc and fire his pistol. As the retrieving dog returns to the handler, the handler presses a remote button, which launches a bird directly in Pup's return path. All of which is an enticement for Pup to drop the bird he has and pick up the one that just popped up. This is the kind of test that really tickles the fancy of the field trial set.

Me? My dogs would try to get both birds in their mouth at the same time and make only one trip.

THE SLOW RELEASER

Some fifteen years ago a Colorado resident got hold of me and demanded he show me his new invention: a slow-release launcher.

His purpose was to have great metal wings open slowly and silently, so the oncoming dog wouldn't hear them, plus the planted pheasant—the pheasant within the device—would not spook and fly away.

What all this presented the retriever was this: The wings opened and *the pheasant walked out.* In every instance the bird just stepped out on the grass and stood there—yes, I went to see it work. Never once did the bird take off, which means the oncoming dog gets to flush the pheasant, just like he would on a day's hunt. And there's no clanking machinery launching the bird to air, and for sure no malfunction where the bird is found within the steel wings due to a late release by the hunter and the dog hurts himself pouncing on it.

THE CHAIN GANG

Now another piece of equipment that should be in your truck is the chain gang. This training apparatus has probably saved more drop-out dogs than any other single device.

It's built like the old picket line the cavalry used to tether their mounts, only we use chain instead of rope. Buy that length of heavy-duty, welded-link chain to fit your pack. On each end weld an O-ring. Now get two circus stakes and pound them into the earth a few yards apart—the length of your chain—then drop the O-rings over them.

Every sixty-six inches along the length of the chain we now attach an eighteen-inch drop chain ending in a swivel snap. The space between drop chains, plus the length of the drop chains, has been tested by hundreds of dog men over many years, and it's been learned no two standard-sized gun dogs can reach each other to fight.

Now you snap-swivel your pack to the chain and stand back. If the students haven't been steadied to the check cord, they're going to leap, thud, dig, scream, bite the air between them and their chain mates until they finally become fatigued, but good, citizens. Plus, they will have learned to give to the lead, just like the litter-box check cord puppies, and no human has been involved.

But that's only one value. More important to us is this is an excellent way to hold your pack in witness to a working dog. The chain gang pack watches the dog work afield, and, man, do they want off that chain and

Three Labs and a Chesie make the chain gang rattle and roll.

into the fun.

This means the chain gang is the greatest stimulating device available to a trainer. Plus, in a way, it lets the handler train several dogs at the same time.

This is the device used to cure a gun-shy dog, a bird-shy dog, a dog that has no enthusiasm for the field. It'll flat put nitro in the dog's heart. Yet at the same time, it'll take the fight out of a kick boxer and get him where he'll work with other dogs.

The only problem with a chain gang is you've got to have several dogs to make it rock and roll. And there continually has to be new dogs on the chain to really make it shake, jerk, and sling. So once again, the pro has the advantage over the amateur. There's always new dogs coming onto his place. Therefore, you get all the club dogs—remember that dog club you joined?—on the chain or borrow your neighbors' house dogs.

Well, that's it. Now we're off to the hunt. You know that I personally don't care if your pup doesn't know scat. I don't want an obedience dog, I want a hunting dog. My mother never did get my elbows off the table, but I've never missed a meal. That's the kind of dog I want for you. Sorry, Mom.

Training/Hunting/ Training/Hunting

*"I have enormous respect for the purity of their character and
the sincerity of their everlasting devotion. Sometimes when I go to the kennel
it saddens me to see these wonderful animals wanting their freedom so badly.
But obviously there is no practical solution to this, so I take them out—
as many as I can, as often as I can—and what a joy it is!"*
—Bob Wehle, *Snakefoot: The Making of a Champion*

You and Pup and I are ready to go hunting. But first, let's tie up some
loose ends you didn't even know were hanging.

TRAINING WITHOUT TIME

In no way are you and I training Pup by a clock or a calendar. That's been
tried and the results were disastrous. What we're doing is giving Pup the
opportunity to develop at his own pace in accordance with his own
natural ability. Remember Camas, Mike Gould's precocious Lab bitch,
was guiding big-buck clients on a game preserve at nine months and
garnering handsome tips for her guides. If Pup can do that, then let him
do it. If not, keep giving him the opportunity until he can do those
things that please both himself and you on a typical day's hunt afield.

For as Wehle reveals above, Pup deserves a good life. Keep him stimulated. There's nothing more sad than a kennel-blind dog. And let me
speak of happiness. I can see the depression, the concern, in my dog's eyes

A golden retriever with a shotgun and pheasant on an autumn day. (Photograph © Bill Marchel)

when things go wrong with them. Dogs fret. They suffer stress. Try to be their protector. You can turn a bad day for them into a good day that same way a caring spouse does for her (or his) mate, or either of them does for a child. Remember the deeper the bond, the more sensitive the dog.

Recall the true story of the dog who loved the railroad man. One day the man did not return. The dog lay beside the tracks the rest of his life at the very spot he last saw the man. Such stories are legion. We're not dealing with an automaton, we're dealing with a very sensitive, bright, perceptive living thing.

Plus, remember our previous chapters. We know a newborn pup is like a soft ball of clay. You can easily sculpt whatever you want; you can imprint what you want; you can mold this dog into many unique ways for life.

But as the pup grows, the clay hardens and it's difficult to imprint. So we provide maximum stimulus to new pups since they are ideally adapted for such overload. Therefore, this is a time to concentrate on Pup, but at the same time you must think deeply on what you teach. What Pup learns at five weeks he keeps for life.

THE BUTT LOOP

Now let's talk about gear.

I want you to take that check cord off Pup's collar and make a butt loop out of it. We're moving our point of contact from Pup's neck to his hindquarters. Why? Well, every time you pull that check cord, you hazard turning Pup's head away from the action, possibly taking him off game.

Here's what we do. Fit a canvas dog collar about Pup's waist. Then swivel-snap the collar's D-ring to the check cord. There'll be no tightening of the collar if Pup tugs, which makes this device a teaching tool rather than one for correction.

You'll need several different-sized collars to fit your string.

When a bird dog with a butt loop goes on point and breaks on wing and shot, the handler holds steady, and the dog doesn't have his head jerked sideways as he hits the end of the rope, losing sight of the bird. Instead, the dog continues looking straight at the fly-away.

Also, when you're working a dog with a butt loop you're not pulling him off scent through his neck collar. His head is free to work scent, and when the dog points the bird you go up your cord, flush the bird, and if the dog breaks to hit the end of that cord, you've got more control of the

German shorthair pointer shows the proper fit of a butt loop.

upcoming jolt. You've got more power.

You old-time trainers will recall one way to get a retriever to drop a bird he's clinched tight is to reach over, hook your index finger inside his flank, and pull up. Pup's locked jaw will open. Our butt loop can be touching that very flank—there's sensitivity there.

TEACHING THE LAB TO POINT OR WHOA

Now right away I want to dispel any notion I want a Lab to point or to whoa and hold steady at the edge of a covey's scent cone. Far from it.

These pointing Labs are a fad right now, and we're all aware of how America loves differences that make no difference. When I was a young man I was a businessman, a city man. It wasn't me. So I left for the outback and went to the dogs.

The dogs and I lived where the cottonwoods stood sentinel, the mixed prairie grass grew high as your belt, and flat-sided bluegill splashed in a wind-capped pond. And with the dogs and all of that, I got to being me.

There's no way to explain it, and yet there's every way to explain it. A dog's selfless love required a payback. As the underdog they were being brutalized in the name of training—and somebody had to stop it. Or try to stop it. So I had my life work, I had my dogs, and I've been happy ever since.

So I'll never compromise with what I think right about a dog or any aspect of dogdom. *A pointing Lab is a sight pointer,* which means he must crowd the scent cone. This further means he's going to be flushing wild birds, while at the same time, he'll be standing there looking straight down at their liberated cousins.

A pointing Lab, due to his caution, lays his nose aside and concentrates on what he can see. Yet that nose is the most valuable tool Pup has; why substitute his eyes for his nose the way field trial people are so fond of insisting?

Also, I'm not interested in training up a Lab that'll whoa at the scent cone and wait for you to come forward. That's fine if you want to hold a covey and train some pups, but that's not very exciting for a day's hunt.

TARRANT'S WILD INDIANS

The joy of my hunting life is seeing a pack of black Labs working bobwhite in a Kansas pasture dotted with crabapple trees, sumac, nettles, wait-a-bit bushes, and a sycamore-shrouded creek bordering to one side.

Those Labs are moving fast and fanatical, leaping each other and sliding slick against each other's hides like dolphins cavorting just off the hull of a great ship. Look at that one jump straight up to get his bearings. The grass is too tall there. See, he's laughing as he casts his head about.

On they surge, sweeping the field with their full-bored noses, knowing contact can't be more than two more leaps away, then WHAM! They plow into the covey and birds erupt like a fragmentation hand grenade.

Don't worry, you're ready *because you can read your dogs.* You knew when they entered the scent cone by the set of their head, the cock of their ears, the tremor of their tails, and you saw Hattie look back for you—that way she always does—silently signaling you to hurry up, "Those birds are coming."

And that's excitement folks. Like nothing else I ever had. The crackling grass stems, the scat of speckled birds, the leap of Shiloh, who's sure he's going to catch two at the same time. The way Thunder stands and arches his spine, trying to grab the backtracker. Or Pepe, who has started plowing the grass roots with his jaw, following a bird trying to leg it out.

Then all the dogs are gathering about you, leaping high with laughing faces to look straight in your eyes, their black hides gleaming, and you see that two have already fetched, then you look down at Pecos for he's pawing your leg, demanding you see the bobwhite he's laid at your feet.

Now if you know a hunt that exhilarates more than that, please call. I wouldn't miss it for the world. But if you don't, then gather up every retriever you can find and head for the fields.

But something vitally important I ask you to recognize. When you put a pup in this melee, he'll come out flabbergastingly happy. Why? Because that's what you've been doing since Pup's first Happy Time walk. *And our Happy Time you'll remember is a no-kill hunt.* So you've been preparing Pup for this covey bust since the day you brought him home. *Hunting is always just an extension of training:* HUNTING/TRAINING/ HUNTING/TRAINING.

Getting Land To Hunt

You see why I want you raising a pack of wild Indians. That's why I prefer to forego yard training or anything that might dampen a pup's spirits, rein in his intensity. But I've got to be practical—for you. Where are you going to find a spread big enough to let a pack go like that? For that matter, where are you going to find a pack?

But that is your responsibility, you know? During the summer you should have been driving the back roads looking for hunting land.

You should have been seeking out fellow retriever men and telling them of your interest in pack hunting bobwhite or whatever bird you seek in hand.

You should have been pulling up to the fence when you saw a guy parked nearby on his tractor, and talking friendly to him. More than that, you should have been asking if there's something you can do for him.

Remember? When you go looking for hunting land, take work gloves, not a shotgun. As the years pass you'll be surprised at the land you gather. I'll bet my buddy, Jim Culbertson of Wichita, Kansas, who's been asking permission to hunt for forty years, probably has a million acres he can access. It builds up fast in 40,000-acre parcels.

All summer long you must keep up this emphasis, forever looking for training and hunting land, forever seeking others of like mind to throw themselves and their pups in with you for maxi-hunting. For it is hunting that pleases the dog. Not some tedium where the dog is always contained and moves only to fill an order you give. But a dog casting with its own lead, playing out its own hunches, bringing deadfall to you that control hunting would never have realized.

It amuses me to recall Mike Gould's critic who chastised him for letting his dogs cast long and wide. "They knock up birds out of range," the man griped, "And you can't shoot that far."

Mike smiled, as he always does, and answered, "That dog did me a great service by knocking up that bird. You see that bird came out of a plum thicket. So now I know where the birds are hanging out, and I'll gather up the pack and hunt the thickets. That scouting Lab saved me from hunting all over the country."

POND JUMPING

All my hunting is not an invasion on quail with the artillery's blare and the rockets glare of a Normandy invasion. There's times the dogs must show discipline: come to heel, be quiet, sit, and stay.

Like when you sneak forward and peer over the pond dam. Yes, there they are. Eight mallards, three pintail, a handful of coots, two gadwall, and one baldpate.

Shiloh as a six-week-old pup. His whole life he was loved to performance. Your pup can be, too. (Photograph © Dee Tarrant)

You hear brittle grass move behind you—someone's creeping forward. You turn with frowning face and wave him down with a flat palm, looking mean. And remember: no hunt is so important you can't stop and train. Plus, the hunt itself is training.

Now you back off the dam and scoot around to the west where most of the ducks are sunning. There, that's about it. Now you turn back and wave an arm for the pack to join you. They come too boisterously, too quickly, but then that's what I raised and that's what I encouraged. "Shhhhhhhuuuuuu," I tell them, waving down with flat palm. "Be quiet," I hiss. They settle, looking pouty, impatient, panting, ready to go.

I crawl back up the dam and see I've got a good angle and right distance for the most ducks. Now I slide the safety off, get ready to stand . . . easy does it . . . don't blow it . . . there! The flight explodes and hangs in air as the crack of the shotgun reverberates among the pond trees and races for the open prairie. Plop, plop, plop, the ducks drop. The Labs have broken, they've cleared the dam and hit the water following twelve-foot leaps.

Look at them churn toward the one they've picked when they crested the dam. Watch Shiloh grab that mallard and spin, his black tail lifted, throwing droplets in a ten-foot arc. Now he's heading home, puffing loud, glancing sideways to make sure no thief intends on dry-gulching his duck.

It's good times. I laugh at the pack's spirit, their happiness. They're doing what God sent them here to do. I am, too.

Brittle Cold, Like Glass

There's so many hunts I enjoy. But they don't all have to be brawls. Those that are silent and easygoing also hold a special place for me.

It's cold, bitter cold, a dull blue bitter cold. The whole country is like glass, just step on it and it shatters. You can't breathe, it's that cold. So I have a muffler across my mouth, and I spit bits of wool lint, and strands of wool stick to my lips.

The dog doesn't know it's cold. He hunts. Hunts hard. Knowing no bird will be sitting atop these piles of snow. Knowing the pheasants have dug in, they're under the snow, and the dog will have to find their telltale blowhole and root them out.

Shiloh turns to look at me, great gray vapors circling his head. He laughs. All Labs laugh. All the time. I tell him he's doing good and that I love him. He casts again, angling right, he'll check some brittle brush along a pond's side.

The silence is deafening. I think deep, beyond thinking. I am walking mesmerized, listening to my hush-breathing, hearing the crunch of my big boots in the crusted snow. A crow tells me I'm nuts, tells me to go home. I swing my gun on him, get him in my sights, drop the barrel.

The dog has seen the gun come up, he's standing locked muscle. Where, he wants to know? How could I have missed it?

I tell him, "It's nothing . . . go on."

Then he has it, he coils back like he's been hit by a swinging door. Then it's all let loose. Shiloh clears the snow and in a great arc sails headfirst into a small drift. "Ack, ack!" screams the big cock pheasant bulldozed from his snow bed. His wings rising high and slapping down hard against his bronze chest. He can't make elevation. The dog leaps and has him, the big bird flapping his wings to hurt the dog, the bird trying to direct his beak to stab the dog.

So Shiloh drops the bird and grabs a wing tip. Now he comes toward me twirling the bird flying in a great arc about his revolving body. No way could I have taught that. Shiloh has logically seen the best way to keep from being hurt by this frantic bird and is keeping the bird at distance. The teacher? Genetics, the way of Shiloh's ancestors eons ago.

Shiloh has just justified his species and his birth. The gray landscape is suddenly brightened without sunshine. I'm so proud of his success— his innovative success.

And I prize being part of some prehistoric outcropping in Pup's strategy. That's more than I hoped for in coming here. For having invested my life in helping you bring along dogs like Shiloh.

I consciously fought to break out of today's humdrum, structured, and spiritless society, to reject plastic, concrete, steel. The neon's jitter, the rude man's shove, the machines acrid stench, the cast-iron culture's paranoia regarding gender, race, religion. Everything is an issue. In an age to pride tolerance, there is no tolerance.

What I traded all this for was to see a tree, pick a grass stem, soak my feet in a brook, listen to a squirrel's chatter, watch a sunset, walk home tired in the dark. To distance myself from man's stupidity in calling manhole covers "people hole covers," or wondering how I'd ever get a wife today when a wink is court-determined to be sexual harassment.

God, how modern man has a penchant to lay aside good sense.

Retrievers in training must be exposed to all weather; this fetching Lab pup is handling an iced-over pond well. (Photograph © Jack Macfarlane)

But Shiloh has twirled his way to my side, and now he drops the pheasant again and goes for its neck. That way he can block the beak, he can hold the head stiff. And he's to the back of the neck so the bird's spurs don't slash him.

I reach past him, telling him how great he is, how pleased I am, and I take the pheasant by its head and wring its neck. Pheasant are great to eat, and this one will be better yet. And I'll never forget the spinning of the bird that blue day in the deep snow and the look on Shiloh's face when he showed me a thing or two.

The Most Powerful Commands

I have a failing. I get so excited about telling you something I forget to mention something else—something important.

There are no two oral commands more powerful than Pup's name and "No." The inflection used to express Pup's name accomplishes every command we've ever learned. And it's one command that will make Pup gulp, will make him cower forward, serpentining his head, searching for a place to move in and be warm and close, a place where he may kiss you, for Pup can't stand to be on the outside. Same thing goes for "No." That's the power of bonding. *A bonded Pup can't stand to disappoint you.*

These two commands are also the first two commands Pup ever hears. And they're at the tip of your tongue the rest of Pup's life.

The Whistle

You'll remember we started out big time with the whistle and had Gary Ruppel blowing it to the gestating pups—and continuing to blow it the rest of Pup's life.

Well, we will, too. But don't think the whistle is neutral of emotion. When you billow your cheeks until they're red and your eyes are slits and you blow so hard you break the pea, Pup knows you're teed. So control your communicating whistle as you control your communicating voice.

There are times the whistle can accomplish what your voice can't, like on that pond dam earlier. A slight toot on that whistle could have accomplished more than my voice in sitting the dogs, bringing them forward, moving them about the pond. And the ducks would not have responded to a whistle like they would if they'd heard me talking.

There are some traditional whistle signals. One long toot means to stop, attend, sit. A long toot followed by a series of pips means to come in.

A Lab on a log and Omar Driskill, steadying his aim on tree, determine a passing mallard's fate in green timber shooting. (Photograph © Charlie Patterson)

A snappy double toot means for the bird dog to cast, if you're hunting a pointer, setter, or continental gun dog. And that's about it. And if you can blow this whistle without moving the pea, you can decoy pintail with it.

DUCK HUNTING

There were seven years I never missed a single, legal day of duck hunting. I don't recall what the seasons' lengths might have been. But if they were each eighty days, then that means I never missed an outing for 560 days.

Other years I could only get in sixty or seventy days.

So when I tell you something about duck hunting, I'm not supposing, nor deducing, nor passing on other reports.

When you take Pup to a blind, the way he acts is up to you. That crap about a dog milling about a blind and disturbing overhead ducks is the report of someone who hasn't hunted ducks. That dog doesn't need to rigidly sit, nor hide under a tarp, nor keep his head down when ducks are decoying.

Ducks are fascinated when seeing a dog about a blind. It goes back to their curiosity about foxes. You know a fox can cavort on a bank and every duck on the lake will swim close to keep an eye on him. The point being that if they can see the rascal they don't have to wonder what he's up to.

In Europe, hunters build a decoy to take advantage of this, though their decoy is a lot different from what you think. A European decoy is a twenty-foot high, eighty-yard (or so) chainlink funnel (called a pipe) with a series of wood wings (called screens) to one side. A little brown, mongrelly dog, feisty and pinch nosed, is taught to walk about each wing, then secretly go to the next one. The ducks leave the lake to follow the dog up the length of the wired enclosure until they're caught. Not a shot fired and the duck-catching dog has captured every duck on the pond. Neat, huh?

If you want to be novel, teach a dog to dance and roll and be innovative on the bank of any pond. The ducks will swim close to see what he's up to. Then you stand and harvest your dinner.

STEADY TO WING AND SHOT

Now if Pup breaks at the sound of your safety and takes off, that's fine with me. You want him to stay, that's fine with me, too. Couple things we do.

Should you have a sunken blind, you'll need to go during the summer and jump down in there and have Pup either lay to side or join you in the pit. We've got to get a handle on Pup. Anytime you lower yourself, Pup thinks you're going to love him. So he's leaping all over you, kissing your face, and you've got a shotgun, a bag of shells, Thermos, and what-all.

Therefore, you go to the blind in the summer prepared to teach Pup that when you lower your body that doesn't mean you are there to trifle with.

Get hold of Pup and push him down, giving that same command: "Down." Hold him until he recognizes you're not playing. Now let loose, saying, "Down." Should Pup start to stand, push him down again. After repetition, Pup will learn this requirement the same as he learns everything else.

Or there is an alternative. My buddy, a professional duck and goose guide Omar Driskill of northern Louisiana and fellow cofounder of the Hunting Retriever Club, screws a huge eyebolt to a piece of plywood and snaps it to Pup's D-ring. When Omar wants the dog to fetch, he releases the snap, Pup leaps from his plywood floor and dives into the flooded timber.

FORCE RETRIEVE

There are certain things I'll no longer do.

Force retrieve has long been a sore point with me—and with Pup. Why train with pain? In the beginning it was thought you should take the dog to a place he'll likely never be again. And that was usually your bedroom, which indicated this Lab, as most Labs, were housed in a kennel.

Well anyway, you used a rolled-up sock for a bird and you enforced pain by pinching the dog's ear with your thumbnail.

And why pain? Well, you've got to get the dog's mouth open to insert that sock, right? So that's the basis of all force retrieving. The dog opens his mouth to say, "Ouch," or opens it to scream, "My God!"

Well, I'll not be a part of it. And that comes after searching the world for an acceptable way to get Pup to open his mouth. I eventually settled on the nerve hitch. That was a cord tied to Pup's leg, then dropping down about his paw, where you looped the cord around two of Pup's inner toes and pulled the remaining length of cord, as you ordered, "Fetch."

THE NERVE HITCH

The value of the nerve hitch was the cord pinched the two inner toes that way a pencil is run through your fingers while someone else squeezes them. The compressed nerves drop you to your knees. But the hope is there'll be no imprint. The dog will have momentary displeasure, which will immediately disappear when the pressure is stopped.

Well, that's not the case. I've seen dog's toes rubbed raw—or cut to the bone—by the cord.

Remember what Bob Wehle said to our retriever group. He said, "You're teaching them to fetch? I thought that was inherited."

Well, I'll only bring along natural retrievers anymore. That means you've picked an intelligent, intense dog that wants to play the fetch game. Throw the ball and the dog pursues, captures, takes to mouth, and hurries back to hand. *The training—and the ultimate fetching—is in the breeding. It's not instilled in the dog through pain.*

THE GENTLE WAY TO TEACH FETCH

If you're lucky, Pup will be a natural retriever. (Photograph © Gary Kramer)

And remember what we discovered before. Scott learned that at no time could a dog be punished during the teaching of fetch. This is easygoing, sensitivity time. You cajole and entice Pup to open his mouth with the "object" presented. You don't force the mouth open, nor jam the "rolled sock," nor in any way manhandle Pup.

You take your time. Always the training comes with play. Pup is happy, positive. Days may pass. You don't care. Pup must voluntarily take this object to mouth, hold it, and give it up on command.

Oh, you can reach under Pup's collar and insert two fingers in his collar. That leaves your thumb in the right position to place in that indentation under Pup's jaw. That'll help Pup hold the dummy in place. Also, groom Pup's mouth, because we don't want any lips pinched.

Should Pup stick on the object, never pull. Instead, push in and twist. This will gag Pup and he'll release.

THE NATURAL RETRIEVER

But who's to say your pup won't just run out, fetch, bring to hand, and that's it? It happens. I hope it happens to you. I hope your dog is a natural retriever.

And not just because it's easier on you. After generations of such dogs, no one will have to be training with pain. Get me? Proper breeding will make instruments of torture something a good trainer will discard.

So I must emphasize an even greater need for good breeding. The best deal is for the fetch instinct to be in the blood. And if not, hopefully you avoid the pup, and the dogs are not bred again.

A brutality trainer can make retrievers out of Labs that have no such genetic ability. In other words, with pain and force they can make a fail-safe retriever. Pity the poor dog. And pity the person who buys a pup out of such breeding. For the performance was in painful training and not the dog's gene pool.

So I say again: Get the pup that God filled to the brim, not the one whelped by parents who were tortured to do what should have come naturally.

THE WHAT-NOT RETRIEVER

Right now I have the delight of my life. An eight-year-old Maltese/Lhasa apso mix named Candy that's the retrievingest fool ever put on earth. She requires a minimum of thirty fetches a day. God, the intensity! You'll see her lying there—you don't know she's spit the ball out and it's rolled under your feet—and she's eyeballing that ball, waiting for you to notice it and throw it.

How can I keep missing her intensity and her intent? The focused eyes, the arched neck, the upraised elbows not touching the floor, the tense, bent rear legs. "Throw it!" her whole body screams. And when it goes, so does she.

Her nature has now become "If you don't keep throwing that ball, I'll die."

And the other dogs in the house? Nothing. Throw the ball until doom's day and you'll go get it yourself.

Why? Because Candy is the brightest dog I've ever known. And there it is again: smart, intelligent, bright.

That's how you teach retrieve. You breed it.

Hand Signals

Candy is also on hand signals. Self-taught, if you will. Her love for the ball (thrown so she couldn't find it) kept her looking back for help. I'd lift an arm left or right, and she'd go that way. That's it, folks. That's taking a hand signal. Damnedest thing I ever saw. Especially recalling the months I'd spend with a good-meaning Lab trying to get him to take a left-handed or right-handed cast.

And that looking back for help, field trialers call that "popping." It's a demerit. It means the dog isn't competent, so he has to seek help. I don't care. I'm glad I got a dog bright enough to know I'm there to give a hand. Bright enough to know she'll save time by having me direct her, instead of her running all over the field. Of course, that's how a hunter would think.

The Ball Diamond

Now there's a mighty easy way to teach hand signals with a ball diamond. Imagine home plate, first base, second base, third base, and, oh yes, the pitcher's mound.

Let's get started.

Put a pile of dummies on the pitcher's mound. Cast Pup. Nothing to it, the dummy is in hand.

Now remove all dummies from the pitcher's mound and put them at first base. Good, Pup brings all those in as he later does at second base and

So many dogs are brilliant. Here the author catches an English setter unlocking kennel gate so she can self-hunt.

third base.

Now Happy Time Pup about and let him shake it all off. Okay, bring him back.

Put dummies at first base, but cast Pup for the pitcher's mound. Hard to do? Keep trying. If it just won't work, put it all away and come back tomorrow.

Eventually Pup takes your blind cast to the pitcher's mound. Blind cast? Yes. *Pup's going after something he never saw fall or can't see laying before him.* He's going on faith in you. Nothing else. Remember this and don't ever lie to him. Never send him for something that he can't eventually get in his mouth.

When Pup crosses the pitcher's mound whistle him down. Remember? One long toot is to stop, wait, and/or sit.

Pup will stop and look at you, lift your right arm, tell Pup, "Over," and walk to the right. Pup will look over at first base and see the dummies, take off running, get one in mouth, and return to you. Hurray! Pup just made his first blind retrieve, took his first hand cast.

Keep at it with dummies at all bases. Won't be long till you have a do-it-all dog.

Hard Going

But one thing I don't want you to do is take Pup to the field and give him some ridiculous blind retrieve to pick up. You know dogs will always want to leave water and go to land. So should you try to drive Pup through an hourglass pinch of water between two shores? If you do, realize ahead Pup's in for a rough time.

Or to cast Pup so he must swim some ten feet from the shore—along the shore.

And let's say Pup's sent fifty yards to swim amidst ice blocks to get a duck that's fallen on land where it curves off to the west. Pup's had that painful and difficult swim where he could have just ran the bank and fetched the duck. What's your predisposition? Do you like to swim fifty yards in ice water to retrieve something, or do you just walk around and pick it up?

And here's the crux of the matter. All tests adverse to Pup's true nature must generally be taught with pain. That's my big beef. Plus, why teach a dog what he doesn't need to know? There's no reason. Unless man wants to show he's in charge. That man or woman who warms to such dog performance shows his or her primary interest is not loving the dog, but controlling the dog.

Or let's say you cast Pup into a hard wind. "To hell with it," he'll want to say.

Now all this is the stuff field trails are made of. Giving Pup hardship tasks and expecting him to do them without failure nor protest. Bull.

Got a duck floating behind an hourglass pinch of land? Get out of the blind, heel Pup, walk him down there, spy the duck and cast Pup as close as you can to make his retrieve. Now the bird's in hand—conservation has been served—but Pup hasn't had to swim through hell.

Got a duck that fell far away and close to shore? Get out of the blind, heel Pup, walk down there and let him leap to fetch. How much more pleasant than you standing there blowing that whistle, swinging your arms, yelling at Pup, hacking away, by forcing him to swim parallel and five feet off shore to get the duck. Ridiculous.

And I hope you're sensing the reality that field trials and test hunts have nothing to do with bird hunting, but instead with man's domination over a dog. Getting the bird's not the test; Instead, it's seeing if man can force the dog to deny his instincts in getting a bird that any sensible hunter and dog would just get out of the blind and go fetch.

This proves what I've said for years: Field trials are not for testing hunters nor hunting dogs. It's a flawed game people play to terrorize a dog into performing some stupid test that in truth proves nothing more than man's sickness for dominance.

Well, that's it. We've trained Pup and we've gone hunting. So what else is there? Plenty. Read on.

Hidden Balks

*"When you finish this chapter you'll feel like you need a decoder ring
and a lie detector to train gun dogs."*
—Author

Do you realize Pup may have purposely avoided some of your train-ing drills since you brought him home?

"No way," you say.

"Don't bet on it," I answer, "I'll show you. See what Pup's doing? He's got his paw on your foot, right? Well, that's Pup's attempt—if noth-ing but symbolic—to take over leadership in the dog/man pack. This vying for Alpha male is an instinctual trait. But more than that it could also be compounded by the litter-box struggle for hierarchy. The peck-ing order—remember?"

"Aw, come on," you say.

"Oh yes," I answer, "I mean it."

SEEING IT IN ACTION

You come through the door and the house pack awaits you. Sure, they're excited; you're their life. And they're leaping and displaying and hanging in midair. But what's this? That one dog always leaps up—we'll call him Bull—and puts his paws on your chest and roots at your forearms with his nose. What does this mean?

It means Bull craves recognition and physical love more than the others and wants you to pay special attention to him.

A three-month-old golden pup with mischief in its eyes chews on a cucumber. (Photo-graph © William H. Mullins)

But it means more. Bull demands you give in to his will by forcing you to touch him. So if you reach out and rub Bull's ears or even push Bull away, the dog's won. So long as you've touched Bull, he's forced you to deal with him. In his mind, he's forced you to single him out and acknowledge he's moving up the ladder to be pack leader.

So how do you handle this? How do you win and not be forceful? *You simply turn your back on Bull.* Your body language is telling Bull he doesn't exist. No longer do your eyes meet, and this is very important. *For the withdrawal of your eyes and turning your back becomes the ultimate downer for Bull.* However, dogs don't hold grudges. Bull will shake it off, wag his tail, go his way—and test you again tomorrow.

So now that you have an inkling how hidden balks work, here's more.

DEMANDING PUP FETCH

I'll give you a blatant example and then we'll run through some of dogdom's more common balks.

In the old days we'd place a dog on the force retrieve table, but now we've kept the table and eliminated the force retrieve. In some pictures illustrating this chapter, you'll see Gary Ruppel use the table to eliminate hidden balks. He and many others also use the table as a place for intimacy with a dog elevated to eye-height; now it's become a love table.

ONCE AGAIN: EYE CONTACT

Mike Gould recently reinforced for all of us at a gun dog workshop the fact that if a dog won't look at you—won't meet you eye to eye—you'll play Billy Hell ever getting him to take-to-mouth whatever you're offering.

Why?

Well, a dog has never succumbed to you until it has relented with its eyes. Dog behaviorists now know eye communication is the primary source of both a dog's power and discernment.

Without eye contact you cannot control a dog. Think back then to the truly bonded dogs you've had. Never once did they cease to look into your eyes. It's the classic picture of the old hunter with his white, walrus mustache and laced-up boots sitting on a log, with the dog at his feet fondly looking up at him.

But the renegades or the dullards, the ones you could never train?

Gary Ruppel is a master eradicator of hidden balks and believes all balks have been caused by handler error. I write of working Pup on the ground, but Gary uses a table when possible. Here a Lab insists on attention, on being touched. (Photograph © Jim Ruppel)

Gary turns from the Lab, maintaining Alpha rank, refusing to let him have his way. (Photograph © Jim Ruppel)

They were always looking away, always denying your presence, always evading the power of your eyes.

Lorus Milne and Margery Milne point out in *The Behavior and Learning of Animal Babies* that puppies fix on features of their mother's face. They have recorded that when a momma-dog smiles, the puppy smiles. Later, the pup attempts to imitate every unique configuration of the mother's facial features, frown for frown, smile for smile.

They also claim that dogs communicate by eye and give as an example a scientist blindfolding his dog with the result that a strange dog enters the room without hesitation. This is not normal behavior for strange dogs—usually they hold back, wishing they were somewhere else, for they realize the house dog has right of territory and they don't know

Gary directs the Lab's face eye-to-eye with a slim, limber "wand." There is no force, just pressing the wand to a cheek to get the dog to face you. (Photograph © Jim Ruppel)

how strong he may feel about it.

Milne and Milne conclude that dogs communicate with visual cues in excess of what we figure. They also postulate that slight movements and quick glances may, as they say, "Do the trick."

However, we realize dogs communicate with their world in a multi-sensory mode: scenting, seeing, feeling, tasting (which I believe is mostly done with the nose), hearing, and extrasensory perception.

THE POWER OF THE EYES

Notice whenever one dog tries to lord over another dog, the submissive dog always looks away, always lowers his head and turns it to side. We always thought—if we thought at all—the "whipped" dog was trying to keep from being bit in the face. But what the submissive dog is saying by averting his eyes is, "Okay, you win, but I'm not going to acknowledge it." This is a hidden balk. And we thought cats were sly.

Sometimes my wife, Dee, comes up with the appropriate term. Observing the attitudes of our house pack and seeing a hidden balk, she termed it "a sneaky-poo." I like that.

BACK TO THE RETRIEVING TABLE

So what do we do with the dog on the retrieving table? Well, we force him to look at us. Not by manhandling his head and twisting it about, but by taking a thin rod, or plastic fly swatter, or something else pitifully weak, and placing it against the dog's off-side face, pressing the muzzle to front.

When the Lab finally relents with his eyes, the handler backs further and further away, making sure the Lab keeps eye contact. (Photograph © Jim Ruppel)

It may take a half hour. It may mean giving up for that session but coming back tomorrow. But the trainer persists, and eventually the dog gives in by turning toward you and releasing his eyes. Once the dog gives you his eyes, he's yours.

And why did this dog give in? Well, he's bullheaded that's for sure. But you didn't fight him to make him sully up even more. You merely applied *soft* pressure, kept everything low-stress, and by constant contact convinced the dog he'd eventually have to turn and face you. And he did. Once they give in, they're yours for life. And there is total transference of this submission to all other training drills.

If you'd been heavy-handed, you'd still be there; such dogs set in for the long haul. And many are never "broken."

So what's important for you to know here is this. If you don't remove these hidden balks, you'll never have a grudge-free dog, a dog that's all yours and lives to please you. A bonded dog, a dog that, like Bob Wehle says, "Will do what you ask because he doesn't want to disappoint you."

THE FRY COOKS

Likewise, there's another reality I want to emphasize. Those fry cooks sizzling those poor retrievers with electric shock collars—if they'd spend more time studying the dog and learning his core characteristics they could take that instrument of torture and throw it away. We're trying to "read" the dog to performance. They're trying to brutalize the dog into blind compliance. We're approaching through the head. They're invading through the hide.

The Major Hidden Balks

Balks occur in many stages and circumstances of training. Also, they appear one day but not the next. It all depends on how the dog feels; is he having a lousy day? Also, please realize the dog knows more about us than we do. He knows if we're on our game, or distracted, or melancholy. He'll test you when you're weak.

Balks come at the handler's side or a quarter mile away. How successful they are depends on whether or not you detect them. They also seem to come early in a training session and are a particular favorite of most dogs during yard training. But I say again, if the trainer doesn't recognize these hidden balks and put a stop to them, Pup will have them as an ace in the hole the rest of his life.

Pup Leaping on Your Back

Not all dogs seeking the Alpha male role will leap toward your face. Many will get behind you and leap on your back. It's the same old gambit as above. The dog is demanding your special attention, *demanding that you touch him.*

Again, if you fall for this ruse the dog has won. What you do is tell the dog sternly to heel and sit. And tell it hard, tell it with full intent. The dog will know the game is up, and he'll heel and sit like an obedience champ.

Or you can bend a knee and lift a heel to gently catch Pup in the stomach as he's standing there. That'll put him down. In doing this never acknowledge Pup was standing there nor that you lifted your leg. You maintain a pose of having had nothing to do with it, which means Pup caused his own discomfort by jumping.

So there's two things you do: *1) never touch the demanding dog* and *2) never punish him.* For if Pup makes you mad, he's defeated you. He's won. And if you hit Pup, you've just shattered your entire no-stress training program.

As Bob Wehle notes in *Snakefoot,* "In the last few years we have finished dogs completely without physically stressing them in any way." Is this important? Well, Bob can't count the number of national bird dog championships his dogs have won. And another thing. In *American Field,* the newspaper bible of the bird dog world, I counted Bob's kennel name, Elhew, 1,400 times in the last Christmas issue. Most of the words were found in pedigrees of dogs bragged about or pups for sale. Are your dogs

This Lab looks across his handler's knees at some distraction, real or unreal. Until the Lab faces front and center, he cannot be cast. (Photograph © Jim Ruppel)

so heralded?

So it's imperative we make the same no-stress claim as Bob. Never in a moment of anger do we blow it all with one swat.

Pup Looking Off

I was with a great guy the other day, who had an equally great Lab. But the dog had been laid up for several months. The man, nevertheless, laid out a hundred-yard blind in high grass and cast the dog. Of course the dog failed the test.

Then the man shortened everything up and brought the Lab to heel and attempted to try again, hopefully to succeed this time.

However, the dog had failed, he knew he'd failed, and he had no desire for another setback.

Consequently, I stood to side and watched the man lean over his dog at heel and, pointing his straightened left hand, say to the dog, "Line, line, line," which is the field trial command and accompanying hand signal for a dog to cast toward a blind retrieve.

But the dog was not attending. The dog was looking immediately over the man's hand at two trucks parked some thirty yards away at an oblique angle. The man was new at this game and cannot be faulted for not recognizing the hidden balk. The dog was new at it too, but he had the benefit of thousands of years of genetic history. This "look away" is all part of the canine's survival-of-the-fittest evolution that placed this particular dog here today.

Eventually the man realized he can't turn the dog's head so what did he do? He cast the dog. To where? Directly where the dog was looking—to the two trucks.

How often I've seen this at a field trial. And the handler never notices. The dog is telling me from yards away he's going to blow the blind, yet the handler, dimwittedly, casts him.

There are two things to note here: 1) a hidden balk, left unattended, always defeats the handler and 2) a dog will always go the direction his head is pointed. He's like an Olympic diver: Wherever the head goes, the body will follow.

The same goes for a dog's body position at heel. If the dog is cantered away from a right angle to the front, he will cast that way. Make sure his butt is at an absolute right angle to the bird he has to find.

To solve all of these look-away problems, note which direction Pup

*Pup will test you constantly; you need to become skilled in recognizing hidden balks—
no matter how cute the pup. (Photograph © William H. Mullins)*

Working a Lab on check cord, the sit whistle is blown, the dog stops and turns about, but looks away. This is defiance. Solution? Walk toward the dog repeating commands. And yes, here would be a good place for the bowline knot. (Photograph © Jim Ruppel)

wants to look, then take him to a long chainlink fence, like at a schoolyard, and set him up so the direction he wants to look is on his fence side. Now he either takes your line or claws the fence.

Another solution would be to canter the dog more to the left, then cast him. Should he run back toward the right—the way he was look-ing—he has further to turn and run. Plus, he's right in front of you. So you catch him quick with a sit whistle—one long toot—and then cast him the direction you want, or even walk out to him and cast him again. The closer you are to your dog the more power you assert.

Should the dog suck back right, then repeat the procedure.

Finally, far afield he will take the line you want.

Now go back to the initial casting line and run it all again. You will eventually win.

But note this as well: Dogs honor hot spots. This Lab may not be balking at all. On the initial casting line, he may have scented the early morning tinkle of a coyote bitch near those two trucks. Such an odor would be overpowering.

Hidden Balk Additions

There are many additions to a genuine look-away balk.

The dog may be at heel then suddenly stand and walk away.

He'll give you the idea he's just seen something or smelled some-thing, or he may put on an act of rubbing in the dirt, or even urinating or dumping. But it's all a ruse. His intent is to break your authority, to forego the command.

Balks Go With the Territory

Now let me interject a thought. It is believed by a few of my colleagues that if you let a dog develop hidden balks, it means you've been slack as a trainer. You've let problems come up without solving them. You've been flat duped.

Ha! There's not a gun dog in a million that won't challenge your authority. Even that one stellar hunting genius everyone gasps about and raves over—even he will pull your leg. It's built into the animal, don't you understand? It's as much a part of a Lab as his otter tail. Plus, that dog beside you is not a product of you alone. He was several weeks in a litter box with his mother. The pups in that box had their influence. Momma-dog got in her imperatives. And then, Pup may also live with other dogs, and they can demand tribute. And so it goes. There's many factors that can influence a hidden balk. It doesn't always mean trainer failure.

Therefore, to see a hidden balk manifest itself in a dog doesn't mean the handler has been asleep. It means the dog is a dog; his ancestors placed in his blood this ruse centuries ago, and it is not natural for the dog to suppress it. Besides it's fun for the dog! It's sneaky-poo.

The Tarrant Correction

You'll see a dog's look-away balk everywhere in the field. You've sent Pup for a blind retrieve and whistled him down because he's off line. You want to give him a hand signal and adjust his direction.

But what's this? Pup's sitting out there looking everywhere but at you. It's like he's analyzing the field, really getting into this hunting thing.

There's not a gun dog in a million that won't challenge you. Even the greatest retrievers will try to push your buttons. (Photograph © William H. Mullins)

Bosh. He's evading your command. So what do you do?

Well, if you can't solve the problem long distance, then you go to the problem. Get moving. Walk out there, ever keeping eye contact. Should Pup keep his eyes averted, call to him. Make him look at you, look at you all the time you walk toward him. Really let it sink in that you've had it with this ploy, and you're going to put a stop to it.

Now comes the Tarrant correction. You tell Pup how disappointed you are in him, then you reach out and clutch him on both sides of his neck by the scruff of his long fur that's there. Now you simply pick Pup up. Pick him up and hold him straight-armed away from you, while you're looking straight into his eyes. And yes, his eyes are directed toward you by the way you're holding his neck.

Now start talking. Repeat your message. Tell him how disappointed you are. Then drop him. Drop him and tell him, "Heel" or "Sit."

Several things have happened here, the most important being you've taken away Pup's legs. Man, horse, or dog, take away their legs and they're yours. Ask any Olympic wrestler.

Plus, Pup has felt your nonviolent power. I first saw this technique in Marine Corps boot camp. There was a small drill instructor at San Diego who was All-Navy wrestling champion at 135 pounds. All the boots in his platoon were larger, but not stronger. A boot gets out of order, the D.I. would halt the platoon, go to the goof-off and pick him up by his armpits and hold him aloft while they talked. Don't you think that wasn't effective. Talk about humiliating.

And now that you've dropped Pup let's solve this problem. Tell pup, "Line," and cast him for your initial objective. Two bits you get it in fewer than two hand signals.

A False Hunt

You can think of all the other ways, both distant and close, Pup can use this avoidance of looking away. A false hunt is looking away. Know what that is? Well, all of a sudden Pup—who has been sent on an assignment—stops his run and drops his nose to start snooping about.

Anything out there? Of course not. Pup's giving it to you again, taking a break. Well, get on it. Get out there and demand to know what Pup's doing. Never give any slack. Do so and this problem will repeat itself again and again.

Walk Pup away from the area and cast him right back through it. If he stops, go get him, walk him off, and run him through the area again. Keep doing this until Pup barges through without playing his game of "Look what I found."

Or go get another dog out of your rig and run him through it. Is there a hot spot there that just tantalizes the dog? If you find that to be the case, then move your test.

BLINKING

There's an opposite problem. It's called a blink. A dog blinks a bird by smelling it, even seeing it, but ignoring it, acting like it wasn't there. You solve this problem by seeding the area with birds. Now cast Pup through the area. Not even Pup can act like he's not seen nor smelled the whole lot. It takes the luster off a dog to know he's been caught being dishonest. You'll see his guilt. And you'll also see a renewal of an honest attempt to get the job done.

YAWNING AS A HIDDEN BALK

Again Pup is at heel, and you're ready to cast him for a mark or a blind. All this comes up in formal training, right? But I never see it while hunting. That's why I want wild Indians. That's why I train by hunting. I don't want sly robots. Understand?

Well, what does Pup do now? He yawns. Now that's innocuous enough, right? Everybody yawns at some time or another. But a fake yawn?

That's right. Pup's distracting you again. If he sees it's working, he may drop his head and sniff, even walk away.

Well, you're better off if he does walk away. For if he sits there and you get his head up and go ahead and cast him, he's going to blow the mission.

So what we must do is this: Walk Pup off, taking him in a wide circle, bring him back to the point of origin, heel him, and the moment you have his attention toward the area you want him to hunt, cast with a boom.

Boom? Yes. Ram him! Always get your body elongated toward the bird you want in hand. Get like a vintage hood ornament. Get long and lean. Have your left leg way out (Pup is heeled on your left), your body low, your left arm low, your hand extended next to Pup's long nose. You're so close that when you whisper, Pup can smell your mints.

You're that close because you want total control.

Now lifting your arm vigorously like you're throwing a bowling ball, boom, "Back," and watch Pup scat. Scat? Yes. Pup knows you've had it with his duplicity. He wants out of there, away from you. Your act has him convinced you could explode.

THE HIDDEN BALKS OF AGGRESSION AND SUBMISSION

I'll let Mike Gould have this one. He says, "Both these balks are usually caused by fear and anxiety of the kennel surroundings and the uncertainty of the training procedure." Mike is thinking of incoming dogs: clients' dogs. Your dog will have no such fear nor anxiety, and he'll certainly feel good about his surroundings. But this is all part of a pro's woe.

Mike, who refers to hidden balks as escape responses, says, "Sometimes poor socialization and lousy home environments lead to both aggression and submission as an illusion. And sometimes they are hard to read and then the pro can destroy the dog by missing the cues.

"I deal with both of them the same way: with firmness and kindness. Surprisingly you'll often see these dogs switch from one attitude to another. Some dogs that show aggression when you first start with them are really very submissive, and before their true colors are revealed, you could have done immeasurable harm by reading them as aggressors.

"The same holds true for the submissive dog. They can be holding in their hostility and let it explode when you're not prepared."

Thanks, Mike. When handling this duo, I meet firmness with firmness and submissiveness with kindness. If the dog growls at me, or slits his eyes and raises his back hairs, I pick him up, hold him before me, and talk to him. Nothing, nothing, defeats a dog like having his legs taken away from him. But when our conversation is finished I don't drop the dog, I gently lower him. Now let him figure that out.

I've taken all the power he's got, ridiculed it, then softly given him back his legs.

You've got to be careful dealing with a submissive dog. Be kind and he turns to rubber, groveling on the ground, licking your boots, looking up into your eyes like he's met his savior.

But you can't train a dog that's turned to noodles.

You've got to have a tense dog, an enthused dog. Therefore, don't ever get mushy with this one. And of course, don't pick him up and shatter whatever resolve he has left.

You've got to have a tense dog, an enthused dog. (Photograph © William H. Mullins)

The best approach is to play-work with him. Throw the tennis ball and let him run and frolic and fetch. When he returns, rave about him, let him jump, as you slap him on his slab side. Clap your hands, get the dog enthused.

But don't overdo it. This dog is always ready to think he won and crowd your leg by leaning into it. This dog can shrivel like a balloon losing air. Be careful.

Eventually you may be able to emphasize the work and not the play. But maybe not. Such dogs are hard to salvage.

BARKING WHILE WORKING

When a dog barks, he opens his mouth. With his mouth open, he may place your wrist between his teeth. Or he may grab at his lead or your hand, or he may even bite your cheek if you're adjacent and the dog's at heel. So you nip this in the bud, only to have it replaced with his averted eyes.

Now this barking is a ruse to break up the session, to get out of work. And it's also an attempt to vie for Alpha authority. But most of all it's a pain in the neck.

Or the barking is a ruse to bite the hell out of you and get away with it.

No matter what, firmly demand the dog "Stop that noise" and drill him with your eyes. Plus, in the future wear gloves when training this guy.

Also, there is the whining dog. Five time, combined, American and Canadian Field Trial Champion River Oaks Corky—with national championships thrown in—was a practitioner of this. Why? Because he loved birds so much, he was pained to keep waiting on the casting line. He cried about it.

It took hundreds of live pheasants thrown from the line to cure Corky. The process was to throw and shoot the pheasant, while Mike Flannery, the owner/handler, said, "No noise."

It worked for years. But when Corky was eleven, Mike forgot to say it one time at a field trial, and sure enough, the national champion Corky whined.

BARKING

Read the dog and then decide how to proceed. Should you intimidate

This black Lab asserts his authority by putting a paw on trainer's foot. Remove foot and tell Pup to shape up and get with it. (Photograph © Jim Ruppel)

him or ingratiate him? The first thing I'd do is place him on the chain gang where he'd have to watch all the other dogs work.

I'd also buzz the chain gang with pigeons. Toss them so they flap right down the row of it. Don't you think this won't bring a change of mind? Here this pup's trying to get out of work by barking, but after several zooming flights of birds he wants to shut his mouth and get in the game.

Or he changes from barking out a grudge to barking out a hallelujah for birds. You'll have to know how to read your dog.

The Dry Shake

Retrievers are always shaking. But now you've given an order, and the dog has walked off to side and started shaking like he has a wet coat or just dusted. Then the dog will extend this shaking balk to an uncommon interest in something laying on the ground. All of this acting is undertaken to get out of doing what you want.

This behavior usually occurs while the dog is seated at heel. You've given a command he doesn't care for, so he stands, walks to side, and shakes.

Be firm. Demand he heel, then quickly cast him hard. Ram him!

Throw out several short marks and run him without interruption. This will stop that shaking nonsense. Or put this dog on the chain gang. Remember: The chain gang is probably your best training tool. It makes disinterested dogs interested, subdues fighters, builds up slackers, and stops barking, for the dog can be kept there all day and how long can he bark?

The Lab tries different approach by leaning into the handler's knee. He does anything to try and take over the training session without directly confronting the trainer; everything is sly. (Photograph © Jim Ruppel)

Whatever is wrong with a dog the chain gang can cure it—especially with successive flights of birds coming down the line. For birds solve all gun dog problems.

LEANING

Leaning as a hidden balk is just a shade off Pup putting his paw on your foot. Usually the dog is standing beside you, you're trying to teach something, and he leans against your leg. Mike Gould feels, "Dogs use this escape as a depth gauge, kind of a dipstick. They like to see for themselves how deep the trainer goes and how sharp he is. Because they are not all that hopeful that the ruse will work, they usually don't resent being adjusted for it and will quickly abandon it."

Mike further says, "Their heart really isn't into this escape (balk), but they feel compelled to try something to establish a little crack in the trainer's armor."

PLAYING DEAD

Once again we're confronted with the type of behavior a condo dog may display upon being sent to a pro. You know a condo dog? He's lived highrise all his short life, seldom seen the outdoors and never the outback. Nothing special has ever been asked of him. All in all he's lived the life of an urban trust-fund baby.

Now here's this pro standing there, looking stern, smelling of no nonsense. So the dog simply flops dead. You're never going to get anywhere with this dog. His interest isn't opposing you or fighting you,

This Lab has gone for broke: stone dead. Such dogs can usually be manhandled like a drunk, and they will not acknowledge they are alive. This is a "condo" dog on his way home, which is exactly what the dog wanted. (Photograph © Jim Ruppel)

which would indicate some spirit. No, he's willing to take any route out. And he cares nothing about his pride. Send him home fast.

THE CHAIN GANG AGAIN

But if you insist, put him on the chain gang and let the other dogs really work him over. For you see, the dogs are all watching you working. You're working a dog out front with bird boys and birds and gun. And it's all as exciting as can be. And those chain-gang dogs want off the bench and into the game.

Consequently, they're rocking and rolling that chain, sending shock waves its full length, jerking, leaping, digging, barking, clawing, and just generally fueling pandemonium.   ♦

At least it will wake up the condo dog. And what's more important, if he does come around, he'll hold no grudge against you. For on the chain gang, it's dogs training dogs.

THE BUTT TURNER

A dog will turn his butt on you, nearby or afar.

Say you want the dog to come to you. What does he do? He turns the other way. His reality is this: If he can't see your eyes, he's broken your power.

And this eye thing—we now know a dog senses your eyes even when you're out of sight. Send a dog over a hill when the wind's blowing from him to you, so he can't smell you. He can't detect your attitude by your body scent. (Note: A dog cues on human sweat, which contains butyric acid. The more you become stressed, the greater the acid, thus the greater Pup's detection of your anger or frustration.)

With dog and trainer situated, post an observer on top of the hill.

You've cast the dog to hunt, but soon after he tops the hill, you turn your back on him. You pretend no interest in him. Know what the dog is likely to do? Quit. He'll come in.

But keep facing the dog, with your eyes fixed "through" that hill, trying to imagine where the dog might be on the other side, and that dog will generally stay out hunting until he finds whatever it was you planted.

Or this happens. A dog is fetching, and you've been staring at him all along. But suddenly you turn your head and start to talk to someone. The moment you break eye contact, Pup may go on his own. What does he do? He drops the bird and urinates on it, let's say, or he just takes off for the creek to get a drink.

Or you may have a retriever that returns with a mark, but turns his butt to you, facing out to go for the second mark. You can assume he's so birdy he can't wait. But the fact is he's not coming to heel. He's not letting you be in charge. He wants to self cast. (And oftentimes with such dogs the love of birds is just too overwhelming.)

You may also interpret this dog's action as creeping. Such a dog heels at the casting line in a field trial, but by the time his number is called to be cast, he's eight feet in front of you.

Also, this creeping results in the handler having a hard time getting the bird from a dog that's just fetched. The more you reach, the more he creeps. And it can be accompanied by sticky mouth.

I had such a dog once. We were being judged by two old men who were out of it. The dog came back with a shot-up bird: the first bird of a two-bird blind. I tried to take it, the dog crept forward. I leaned forward, grasping. Finally I got hold and pulled, only to get half a bird, which I gave to the bird boy. It was really shot up.

Now I insisted this dog heel, and when he was at side I cautiously

What mischief lies in the minds of these three Labs? You will know soon enough. (Photograph © William H. Mullins)

reached down and pressed the half-bird into his mouth and twisted, gagging him so he'd release. Good, I got it.

But when I handed this second half-bird back to the bird boy and started to cast my dog for the second blind, one of the befuddled judges said, "Good job."

What? I couldn't make it out. I turned to ask, "What did you say?"

I was told, "That was a good job. You're excused."

But the other judge fumed up, blurting out, "But he's only brought in one bird."

Whereupon the initial spokesman said, "Oh no, I personally saw him take two birds from that dog's mouth."

The dog and I wandered off mumbling, and the bird boy didn't have to plant the second blind for the next dog. It had never been fetched.

So what do you do to correct this creeper? Go to his side, tell him to heel, and walk him back to the casting line. Try to cast him for the bird again. Should he creep, then bring him back and attach a check cord. Should he break with the check cord to hit the end of the line, tie him behind the casting line attached to a stake, tree, whatever.

Now bring another dog up and work the mark. Let the creeper really suffer—and he will.

Finally you can release the creeper and he'll stay. It just takes time—maybe days.

The Butt Displayer

More about the bona fide butt-displaying dog sent to fetch? You walk around and confront the dog eye to eye. If he's got a bird in mouth, take it. If he's not yet picked one up, you walk him to it and order, "Fetch." In either instance you heel the dog back to the casting line where you take the bird in hand.

Now you have the bird boy (if you've got one) replace the bird afield. This time you don't cast the dog as usual, but take off walking, asking him to heel. When you get five feet from the bird, you order, "Fetch." The dog will bound forward, take the bird in mouth, and run back to you. What happened? He didn't give you his butt.

Keep repeating this fetch. Only each time stop walking sooner, until finally the dog can be sent and you stay at the casting line. He will then retrieve and not give you his hidden balk.

Now, as we noted throughout this book, dogs are very conscious of place. If possible, the next time this pup gives you his butt, return him to the same spot where you challenged the balk earlier, and run the exact test again. The light will come on.

THROWING A BIRD

Another technique to cure the butt-displaying dog.

You get ready to throw a bird by clutching it in hand, head-out, then dizzying it—that same way you turn the crank handle on a vintage car. When the bird is dizzied, you toss it sidearm so it flies low, which minimizes the distance it must fall, and therefore, lessens the likelihood the bird will be injured. Ideally, you throw the bird just above and finally into heavy cover, the cover slowing the speed of the bird and finally settling it to earth.

The high cover is also vital to keeping the bird planted. Birds thrown in low cover can see you and the dog and are more prone to fly away.

You who have seen birds planted or planted them yourselves know the bird's head is usually tucked under a wing, then laid in the cover with the head-side to earth. But in tossing a bird to heavy cover, it's not necessary to tuck the head.

At a retriever field trial, the bird boy takes a pheasant from the crate, spins it as described earlier, then tucks the head under one wing and, spreading the tall grass, plants the bird and adjusts the grass about it. This bird is dizzy. He's feeble, possibly nauseated, and disoriented. So he lays there to revive his senses and along comes a flushing dog to raise him to flight.

Flushing dog experts, like those the springer and cocker people invite to their trials, can actually plant a bird for whatever length of time the judges want. Plant it hard, they say, or plant it soft. Phenomenal.

THE PIGEON

Okay, here's what we want for the butt-displaying dog. We want to present a pigeon by dizzying it, keeping the butt-dog at side, then sling the bird, and let the dog break to fetch it. Now there's no dawdling on the dog's part, is there? The dog is animated now. "Give me another," he says.

So once again, there's not a problem that can't be solved with a bird. Right?

But there's an old maxim in dog training. You can't solve one problem without creating another. Now we got a dog that breaks on birds. So

If you bond with Pup, hidden balks will not be an issue. (Photograph © Kent and Donna Dannen)

we go back for a refresher course on stay.

THE SLOUCHER

The sloucher is a dog that collapses at heel. He also sits as he pleases, angled off to side, facing whatever way he wants. Well, this dog can be squared away in but a moment.

The most effective correction is one that comes as a total surprise to Pup. You're standing there, the dog is at sloppy heel, he feels he's getting away with it, and you say nothing. But you ready yourself to lift your right foot (the dog's heeled to the left), which you bring around behind your left leg, and catch Pup on his butt with your boot heel.

But remember, *you had nothing to do with this.* You're standing there looking off distant, you are stoic, you are not involved, you're not even thinking about the dog.

Don't you think Pup won't be confused?

Now he's antsy. No longer slouched, he's up and tense, getting ready should the boot heel come again. Now this is exactly what you want in a heeling dog, so cast him.

I said you could win this one in a second.

CONCLUSION

But is there some blanket way we can dispose of most hidden balks without them ever surfacing again?

Yes, with live birds.

Remember, there's not a problem that can't be solved with a bird. So it stands to reason, there's not a problem that'll come up if the dog is buried in birds.

Dogs were placed on earth to find, fetch, and eat birds (along with some furry varmints).

Birds are their manifest destiny, their reason for being.

It doesn't cost you a nickel to empty your coop and run Pup on pigeons until he's stepping on his tongue. Try the same thing with dummies and you'll get a dog planning a hidden balk.

Likewise, a bonded dog isn't going to con you. He's open with you, for you're open with him. There's no duplicity. Include your retriever in everything you do. Let him know he's your second son or third daughter.

I have such a dog right now. If she goofs and we both know it, her eyes grow downcast, her mouth dries, and she is quick to kiss, even to excess. She has to make up. This thing that's come between us must be removed.

So there'll never be a hidden balk with a bonded dog, unless you've so worn him out working afield that he attempts a ruse just to get a moment's rest.

Also realize this. That pup you raise is not going to be thinking about hidden balks. He's not a condo dog. Plus, you've always been up-front with him, he trusts you, and more than that, he loves you. Those hidden balks are more likely to appear when you buy a two-year-old retriever, let's say, since you think he has potential that's never been tapped. And then watch out!

Now let's take Pup through some drills he'll need to know on a typical hunt.

Let's go.

Hunting Pup Wet and Dry

"A migrating goose, staking two hundred miles of black night on the chance of finding a hole in the lake, has no easy chance for retreat. His arrival carries the conviction of a prophet who has burned his bridges."
—Aldo Leopold, *A Sand County Almanac*

Let's think about Pup hunting in water. What are the temptations, the hazards? I can think of many just in a split second: getting in and out of a boat, becoming tangled in decoy lines, thinking a decoy is to be fetched and then dragging it ashore, not fully understanding sheet ice and breaking through and getting stuck under the ice, stepping on broken glass, having an encounter with a water moccasin.

Just this grouping should get us started.

DECOYS AND BOATS

Both decoys and boats should be introduced on land. Lay out some decoys and let Pup accompany you through them. When Pup starts to fetch tell him, "No," then offer him a treat, if that's your nature. Dried liver is the all-time favorite.

And the landlocked boat? Tell him to enter over the side, while you're sitting inside to tempt him. When Pup has his front legs over the gunnel, reach out and push down gently on his neck, and his body will follow into the boat.

It's also necessary you take Pup for many varied boat rides, say in shallow running water where you both get out and portage a sand bar;

A hunter and his Lab watch for ducks on the edge of a marsh. (Photograph © Bill Buckley/The Green Agency)

various depths with high winds raking the surface; even capsizing a boat, then keeping Pup from hindering you as you right it. Can you imagine righting a boat with a sixty-five-pound retriever on your back?

And did you know some dogs can't swim? They are head-rearers. They splash a little water in their face with their front paws, so they raise their head. When they do this they lower their butt. Now the front legs are completely clear of water and they really splash a tossed sea, which means Pup rears his head even higher, lowering his butt even more.

Well, to stop all this, come along side Pup in a boat and reach over, shoving his head down. This will lift his rear end and submerge his front legs, and Pup will soon note and correct his fault.

Or you can do it just standing in the water and catching Pup as he goes by. Beware of his toenails; they cut, and Pup is pumping with great force.

ANCHOR CORDS

Decoy anchor cords are an aggravation. The same guy who invented them must have invented tangled clothes hangers and speed bumps. My argument with decoy cords is everybody ties them too long.

Plus, I hunted so much in Kansas, where the state's name is taken from the Kansa tribe—and Kansa meant in their language, "The South Wind." It should have been, "The Strong South Wind." So my decoy cords were always stretched out. Plus, they naturally got tangled. So when Pup would get hung up with one string, he'd drag the whole layout to shore.

I never did figure out what to do with decoy cords, but I helped my pups get through them. I'd put out decoys on a hot summer day, take the pups to water, and let them swim around the stretched cords. When they got caught, if they panicked, I'd simply help them with the mess. None of this was ever allowed to become a big deal, and we never had a bad incident during duck season.

The only thing I did do that helped was buy some plastic-coated wire, heavy enough to be semi-rigid, and tied it to the decoys and weights. This wire was too heavy to tangle easily, and it really reduced the number of tie-ups the dogs experienced.

FIVE-STRAND BARBWIRE FENCES

Fences can be lethal. When you have five strands of barbwire they are

Dragging wing, a Chesie pup finally pulls duck from boat. Pup should get used to boats on land first. (Photograph © Butch Goodwin)

usually strung tight enough, and assuredly they are close together enough, for a dog to get hung up in them. That's when you need a pair of wire clippers or a set of those Leatherman survival pliers.

Each year there are dogs (especially bird dogs) that die tangled up in a barbwire fence. Either the owner doesn't find them in time or he hasn't got the tools to free them.

When working to release a hung-up dog, don't get close to him. Dogs can become frenzied after they've fought to free themselves a long time and failed. You get close, and you'll likely get bit. Just cut all the wires and let Pup drop to the ground wrapped in the mess. Then immobilize him with a blanket tossed over him, and as you control and settle him, another hunter can remove the wire.

Also, when hunting and Pup is running free, get him in hand before a barbwire fence, then settle him down. Lowering yourself to one knee, shove Pup under the bottom strand of barbwire. A few drills like this and Pup should learn to always go through a fence on the ground—not in the air.

A retriever going full-bore might not see a fence coming. Make sure you have the tools to cut Pup free. (Photograph © Bill Buckley/The Green Agency)

First-Aid Kit

There are all kinds of reference manuals—some even fit in your hip pocket—that will teach you basic first aid. I mention it here because it's imperative you have both the instructions and the kit.

There's never been a season hunting that I've not had an injured dog. The outdoor world is set up for it. A big wind tears loose a chunk of galvanized roofing, then it's left concealed in the tall grass, and here comes my dog to ram into it. Now we've got to sew the dog up or get to a vet and have him or her do the job.

Ever read about my pup Happy, whose stroke of a front leg while swimming drove a huge trotline fishhook through his ankle? And I was out there in water, holding Happy back, trying to cut that line. We made it.

If you don't get a kit today and put it in your hunting rig, you're just telling Pup you don't give a damn about him. I guarantee you, that kit is going to be needed.

Potable Water

It's imperative you carry water in your rig. You don't just need it for Pup to drink, you need it to wash up and especially clean Pup's eyes after he's hunted through a row crop for pheasant.

You won't believe the gunk that will puddle to the side of his eyes. Then you wick this away or brush the rough stuff off with a Kleenex or soft cloth. Neglect cleaning Pup's eyes and next morning you'll have a bug-eyed dog, extremely nervous and sidetracked due to irritation caused by the accumulated debris.

Ears require equal inspection and care. You'll never imagine what you're going to find in there. However, never try to retrieve something lodged deep with, let's say, a pair of forceps. It's imperative you leave extracting such debris to the vet.

Dog Boots

I've hunted extensively in the desert where everything is designed to cripple you and Pup. So this is a place your dogs can use some hunting boots. The boots come in all materials and designs. But here's a warning. I recommend you buy them right now, when Pup is first venturing out into the world, so you'll have Pup used to them when he runs in prickly country.

If you wait until the first morning of legal hunting season to put boots on Pup he'll glomp around all day—wasting his hunt—because he's disturbed by those boots. I've seen dogs with their paws higher than the hooves of a Tennessee walking horse. It looks like Pup's trying to extract himself from a Jell-O dessert.

If Pup objects to hunting boots, then coat his paws with a mixture called Tuf-Foot or something of that sort. Yes, this stuff helps. And why do you need it? Well, such applications can help some with awns, goat heads, stickers, cacti thorns, and running briar, but they are especially good for keeping Pup from shearing a pad on a slab of rock and ending his hunt for several days.

ODDS AND ENDS

Never, never haul Pup about in a pickup bed nor in the trunk of your car. Yes, I know they've come out with chains or lines now that can seemingly anchor Pup in a truck bed, but still, he's more likely to be hurt there in a wreck, and for sure he's taking a beating from the wind when you're going seventy miles per hour.

The car trunk? Bad deal. Too stuffy and too much chance for carbon monoxide poisoning. If Pup isn't good enough to ride in your car, then you've got a real problem.

Whatever way you transport Pup inside your rig, pad the floor so he doesn't take a banging. Use bed covers, towels, rags, rubber mats, cushions, whatever.

Always carry Pup's standard diet with you afield. Feed him anything else and you can have a case of the scours. That can be bad enough afield, but I'll tell you from experience, it can be devastating when you've invited Pup to spend the night in your motel room. "No Ma'am, I have no idea how that stuff got there. What is it, anyway?" I remember once swinging out of bed barefooted to find "it" by touch.

Also, please check Pup for ticks and flies. It goes back a long time now when we'd never heard of Lyme disease, but the rheumatoid arthritis I have may have been caused by ticks (or flies?). Carry both a bug spray of the right concoction plus a pair of "removers" that magically lift ticks from the hide with no fuss.

I've been around too many stoved-up, arthritic warriors afield. They want to hunt, their flanks trembling, their cataract eyes watering, their whole body begging you to wait for them. My heart goes out to them. If there's any way you can, help them avoid arthritis, or should they have it, keep them comfortable.

HEARING LOSS

And then there's this. I don't know how you're going to keep a duck dog from going deaf from noise-induced hearing loss. There are just too many shotgun shells fired right next to his ears; it's pretty close working in a duck blind. But you can at least wear ear plugs and help yourself.

You know I'm always doing things doggy, mostly with no good news for results. I had a magnificent old Lab who'd gone deaf. Not with me, but with another guy, and I bought the dog. Well, I figured there had to be some way to get through to this dog, so I bought an electric-powered megaphone. When Pup was far afield, I whistled to get his attention, he turned, then I shouted in the megaphone, "Come here," and Pup bolted off the training grounds. He was thinking, "Who in the hell is that guy with the spooky voice?"

Lesson? Dogs just won't let you alter yourself. You've got to walk the same, sound the same, smell the same. Plus, that different voice—pups just don't like anything new.

Now who's for going duck hunting?

Of the Hunt, By the Hunt, For the Hunt

"This is written for the luckless ones who have never stood,
gun empty and mouth agape, to watch the golden needles come sifting down,
while the feathery rocket [ruffed grouse] that knocked them off sails
unscathed into the jackpines."
—Aldo Leopold, *A Sand County Almanac*

Have you ever gone to one of those 136-item buffets with maybe ten theme stations, plus a salad and dessert bar? Well, that's how I find duck hunting. There's always another entrée, another snack to try.

To me, duck hunting is a religion, or at least a ritual, enveloping many things: wind choruses, pastoral paintings, bird ballets, murmurs of water on the bowed side of your boat, the fascination of duping the most leery of the wild to enter your trap.

I love the dark when laying out decoys, the strange sounds and musky odors, the water pressing on my waders. The call of unknown, fragile shore birds having to wake up and go to work one more day.

Then the first ducks rising from the refuge and heading for their favorite grain field—great skeins of them, far off, black rivets in an aluminum sky. And watching the wind try to pick the cotton out of ragged cattails. Catching sight of three mud hens passing through the narrow passages of water weeds. And a black spider weaving a web six inches from my face.

Waterfowlers returning from a morning hunt. (Photograph © Lon E. Lauber)

Then there's hearing the old Lab's complaint, for he's saying, "The sun's been up five minutes, and we don't have a duck in the blind."

So I reach out and grab that cape of muscle bowed about his neck, and feel him shift his body weight, glance at me with impatient eyes, lick his chops. He's saying, "We come every day. Can't you ever set up where the ducks fly?"

The gun rests cold in my lap and hands. It's ready. It just looks idle. It can come up and do its work as fast as a charwoman chasing a cat with a broom.

"Hush," I say to Pup. He whimpers some more, for the ducks are before us, aimed straight at us. Eight of them. And they're looking, considering. Then the lead duck angles abruptly high and to the left, circling the blind but still critically considering it. I let them go. Pup is cold stone.

Then they return; the old hen has been duped. She tells her klatch, "It's fine here . . . we'll sit a while." But they're met with the model-12's blow, and three relinquish their reservations in South Texas for the winter.

Pup fetches them to hand, and I sit in dawn's light, marveling once more at the intricacy of their brilliance, that magenta, wine, bronze speculum, the colors sliding and changing with the sun. Then I lower the ducks to hang from the milk stool I use and find a stick of gum to wet my mouth.

That's duck hunting—or part of it. There's training the retriever, and making your own decoys and then repainting them each summer, and raising tall grass to make your own wraparound duck screens. There's learning to blow the duck calls, keeping keen with your gun by practicing skeet, and planting wapatoo, duck potato, and Japanese millet if you have a place of your own, making a mecca for migrating waterfowl.

There's so much; duck hunting is endless. For no two hunts a year have to be alike. And no two hunts in a lifetime really are.

RIVER HUNTING

Pup and I float the Arkansas or the Ninnescah rivers, low-flowing prairie streams in Kansas, sculpting the landscape as they incise and meander. We hunt them in the winter, with ice on the surface, since ducks seek open water near a great cutbank and rest there knowing they'll not be seen nor disturbed. The bank and the ice are their protectors.

Pup rides to front in the bow, his head stuck even further ahead to see around the next bend. Of course, his head can't stick out that far, but he tries. The water lounges beside us, making no sound; it's so eerily calm I can see reflections of red-tailed hawks in the water as they pass above us.

Of course, with no current I have to paddle. Yes, another hunter would be nice.

On the banks there's occasionally late-blooming sycamore, white-trunked, to angle from the bank with great five-point, brass leaves. The cottonwoods are everywhere. The goal of this hunt is to catch a current—there is none today—and float the river, bushwhacking the dozing ducks, then casting the dog to fetch, and helping him back in the boat as you pass by the scene of the harvest.

The only thing that can beat it is to float a great desert canyon river and cast the dog up the high cliffs where he encounters and bumps chukar to flush and glide to the river, where you sit in your boat and take them.

Or like today, bank your boat, call your dog, and go find that pheasant you just heard squawk. Or if you're bored, just let the dog loose to run the bank and knock the Oriental bird up and possibly have him fly across your floating path.

Still yet, break out your spin set and cast for channel catfish, bass, or maybe bluegill. But know this. You should practice this at home without hooks, for Pup will want to fetch whatever jumps at the end of your line. Then when actually fishing, use barbless hooks so if Pup insists on bringing in the catch he won't get snagged.

Bank your boat, toss out your grill, build a stick fire, get vigorous with some Shake n' Bake and share lunch with Pup. The late M. Wayne Willis, famed outdoor artist and my back-country buddy, would always carry beer on our hunts, and I admit, marinating the fish with beer helped the fish fillets.

WHY I'M DOING THIS

So what's the reason for all this reminiscing? Well, it's my pleasure and I thank you for letting me step inside for awhile, but more than that, it shows you the many things Pup must be trained to do before you ever reach for your gun.

Anything mentioned above could be a calamity with an untrained pup. Yet with an old pro it becomes the outing of a lifetime. So why put

A golden swims hard for a retrieve in a Minnesota marsh. (Photograph © Bill Marchel)

up with the aggravation of a dog who doesn't know scat? And you can avoid that just by having the dog in your house, at your side, and forever in the field as much as you can.

I repeat, dogs learn by osmosis (FIDO). Store your wedding suit in mothballs and nobody will sit next to you at your uncle's funeral. Mothballs are potent; their smell is in the body of the suit. Bond with Pup and your influence will be equally permeated. The essence of you will be embedded in Pup's psyche.

OTHER HUNTS

No telling where you and Pup will be invited to duck hunt. For I'm going to tell you something—get an all-age dog and you'll be receiving hunting invitations from all over. You've done what your wife thought was impossible: You've moved into the social set. Hell, the mayor may be calling you next week for some lake research for the waterworks.

I've been a guest on a Mississippi delta barge that slept thirty hunters. We'd disembark in pirogues, manage a mile or so of that treacherous river, cut inside through the small islands of cover, then back our craft into great green tuft. The chatter of nutria dentures rattled in the bush. Pup wanted to stay, but I really didn't care to learn how well he'd do with a twenty-pound rat.

Also, never forego an outing on Chesapeake Bay where big-time duck hunting was born. Oh, you'll not be going out in layout boats nor sneak boats like the old days, but you can get into some productive point shooting. You know, you set up on a point of shore raked by prevailing winds, lay low behind some driftwood, and wait for the ducks to scud by. Pup will be in his element here.

Don't forget the pond jumping either. That's fast and furious when you find it. And do the retrievers get excited. You only have to introduce a Lab, golden, or Chesie to something one time, and he will remember it for life. That's why training errors can be so bad. Pup won't forget if you blow it. So sensitivity training buffers this for you, helps protect you. Remember.

TRAIN BY HUNTING

I guess what I want to say is this. Work with Pup every chance you get, if not for your sanity, then for his. Not to where it becomes boring—always leave a session with Pup on an edge. "End with a sweetener," we say.

Then when hunting season opens, ask your wife's (or husband's) forgiveness and take off. Try to enjoy every day possible, for here is where Pup is really trained. Remember Ben Williams: "Why teach a dog what he doesn't need to know?"

Well, we're hunting now. Everything pup is doing *he will need to know for all your tomorrows.* So this is maxi-training time, full productivity training time.

If you stand in your backyard and throw dummies and tell Pup to heel, sit, stay, you may think you're training a gun dog, but you're not. You're training a very dull automaton. Matter of fact—and you'll have to agree to this—you're training a dummy dog.

For what does all this mean to Pup? Can he translate this into adventure? Of course not. He doesn't feel the fever rise in you as you raise the gun, nor does he smell the smart, acrid scent of gunpowder and hear your voice yell, "Get him, Pup!"

What bird has Pup seen but a sparrow? Imagine the adrenaline in him when the first pheasant squawks or the first flight of ducks hits the water.

But just you and Pup in the backyard playing dullsville will destroy Pup, not make him. Matter of fact, it can easily make what we call a "boot licker." That's a dog who doesn't know scat and is always under your foot afield.

Remember, you can't train a bird dog without a bird.

So do it!

Get the birds, grab Pup, get out of that backyard, go to country where he can smell cow pies, hear the coyotes howl, see the bull kick dirt in a high arc.

Get him into life. His life.

You may be of the city, but he's not. He's your ticket to outdoor adventure.

POSSIBLY THE GREATEST HUNT OF ALL

Notice I keep describing hunts. Well, I'm hoping you'll be so intrigued you'll grab Pup and go. For that's when he will be and where he will be trained.

And the most exciting duck hunt you'll ever make comes about through pre-hunting. Matter of fact, most hunts come about through pre-hunting. For days and weeks you drive the country, glass the fields,

Retrieving a mallard. (Photograph © Bill Marchel)

hoping to find a pattern. You locate a feeding flock of waterfowl, learn where the flyways are, memorize the country.

Then finally there it is. Probably about four o'clock in the afternoon and some distance from the road. There's a large flight of mallards raiding a row-crop field. They're a mass of black dots. Lower the car window and you can hear their feeding frenzy. There's nothing like it.

For once you get back to that field at three o'clock the next day, and you and Pup sneak in there and find a place to lie down, both of you could likely go to sleep, slumbered by the soft wind, the rustle of brittle leaves. Then all hell breaks loose. A great approach of thunder, a cloud that blackens the sun from the sky. They're on you.

You can't believe the power of it, the bedlam of it. These ducks are obsessed. They're saying, "This is only 640 acres of feed, and we've only got fifteen minutes to eat it all."

You shoot, a duck falls. To what consequence? I mean it. The ducks don't care. They continue to dive-bomb. Here comes three, shoulder to shoulder, walking up a row of milo, or corn, or whatever. And what do they do? They hop over you. That's right, they hop over you. Pup is frantic, these ducks have no respect. So he leaps and grabs one in midair, and you must shout to make him release it. And the ducks rioting above do not hear your voice. And there is no way you can shoot them away. The gun means nothing to them.

TEAL

There are two more hunts I want you to take. Let Pup learn two more lessons.

Again you've scouted the country and know what's happening. Finally you've located a flooded weed-seed field where the teal hit at dusk. This is finite shooting. You've got to note the clock and trust your watch, for you're at the brink. Those birds may not give you five minutes of action before they become illegal.

But what shooting!

Again the ducks come pell-mell, careless, reckless. They'll knock your hat off, nearly collide with each other. For they're flying straight into their bed and breakfast. That's right, eat a while, sleep a while.

Maybe there's three of you, which means a lot of fetching for Pup. Bang, bang, bang—he's running. He's spinning, another splash catches his eye. He comes back with two in his mouth.

Everyone's laughing. Hunting is so good.
And you're making a gun dog.
Not in your backyard.
But in the field with wild birds.
Don't forget it.
Make Pup one in a million. Give him all this.
And last of all, take him wood duck hunting.

WOOD DUCKS

It's a woody river, why else would you call ducks that go there wood ducks? So you've got tons of windfall to step over, a thousand low branches to scrape your forehead. It's usually damp; a thick canopy of leaves and limbs deny the sun, so nothing ever dries there.

And here you come glomping in the mud, glassing the vistas. That's right, you need binoculars to look far downstream. For as bright as wood duck are in hand, they're fitfully camouflaged when floating on a stream.

Pup's hunting, too. Running to the bank and looking both ways, sniffing the fetid earth, looking treeward for the chattering squirrels. Later he tries to dig a pack rat from under a tree.

Finally you spot five wood ducks lazing on the stream. Away from the bank you hasten, up into the fields so no sight nor sound of you will come to the prey. You hiss at Pup, "Shuuuu. . . ." He knows what you mean. You also tell him in hushed tone, "Get behind me. . . ." And he does, for he's learned all sorts of words at home.

Now the two of you come sneaking, damning the limbs that slap back from your passing, the ones that poke you in the eye, the ones that Pup—whose now gone ahead—leaps only to have them whip back on your knee and nearly collapse you.

Now you're there, easy. Glass the area, where did they go? There they are. Easy. Get back from the bank and approach again.

Now you've arrived and they are yours, just as a kingfisher spies you and starts yelling it to the world. You hurry, stepping forward to flush the set, and as they rise you swing to hit a small tree trunk and get off only one shell. But a duck pitches to the left and dives at a 45-degree angle to the far bank. "Back," you yell at Pup and he's off.

Then you wait for what seems hours. Finally he appears, laughing, the wood duck in his mouth. It's a drake. Good. More supplies for tying flies. Then you take the bird to hand, smooth its feathers, reach out to Pup and place your hand over his muzzle, thanking him. Suddenly he leaps back, whining, saying, "Enough of that. Let's go."

And you heave up from the log to obey his command and follow him upstream.

You've finally made a master hunter. Ever notice how dumb men say, "I'm going to take my dog hunting?" Well, you say it correctly, for you now have the dog to make the sentence right. You say, "My dog is going to take me hunting." See the difference? It's a difference between night and day. It's the difference between retrievers trained the Tarrant way, and those denied retrievers, who are even today trained to do things that don't matter, while the stuff that counts—the essentials of the hunt—never gets their attention.

WRAPPING IT ALL UP

So what did we do in this book that differs from all other books? Well, we trained the retriever by hunting, which means we had to separate out the individual requirements of each hunt.

For wood duck hunting, Pup had to trail the hunter, keep quiet, stay

Is Pup to be a hunter or an amusement dog? You have the ability to choose Pup's fate. (Photograph © Tara Darling)

A black Lab on a snow goose hunt with rags for decoys. (Photograph © Bill Marchel)

low, and fetch deadfall apart from the hunter's help. So those are the things we train on, not standing in the backyard throwing a dummy or hacking Pup with whistles and hand signals to get a blind.

Floating an iced-up river for mallards, Pup had to mount a boat, learn to ride without capsizing, cast over the gunnels, fetch, and find his way aboard to deliver to hand.

He also cast to shore to hunt up pheasant and hopefully lifted them for the gun. He even had to climb a steep mountain, hunt rimrock, and shoo chukar down to gun range.

Then there was that one hunt that defied every rule. You're lying on your back in the row crop while gluttonous mallards raked the place. And Pup was let go free, to leap from the stalks and snatch at the low buzzing kamikazes, and you fired without consequence, for though a duck would fall, hundreds would take its place in a free-for-all that defied every rule of nature you ever learned.

There was no caution, there was no retreat from imminent danger, you couldn't blast them away. It was riotous and every retriever deserves one go at this during his lifetime.

And that day you walked Pup in the mounded snow, where the wind had drifted to cover the tall grass. Nothing could have looked more unproductive. The land was frozen, barren, without vegetation. And yet Pup persevered, because he had faith in you. And suddenly he scented that pheasant's blowhole in the snow and he dove, launched into a great power arc that exploded into the bird's blowhole. And up the pheasant came, up sputtering, and trying to beat its wings, and ogling Pup with gawky eyes.

How, tell me, could have running blinds in a park or throwing bumpers at a dog club meet prepared Pup for that bird? That's always the point. Is Pup to be a hunter or an amusement dog, a whatnot field trial dog that masters meaningless tests that have minimal adaptation to hunting a bird?

And you see now how Happy Timing Pup with the pack readied him for the riot squad that lifted one covey of quail after another.

Is that enough for you to see my plan? To see why I wrote this hunting book as a training book? To see how the book, then, fits your needs and Pup's requirements more than any other? Oh yes, heel, sit, stay has its place. But it's not all of hunting dogdom. We needed it when we asked Pup to remain behind the dam while we pond-jumped the ducks. Remember? And we needed it again when we shooed Pup and told him to get back from the river on the wood duck hunt.

I'm not saying discipline is without merit. It has great value. But I would never teach it where it stifled a hunting dog's spirit, where it interfered with intensity, thrust, and enthusiasm on the hunt.

Not Done Yet

Consider the work skill required of Pup for each game bird you seek, always under unique conditions. Standing in a bare field drilling Pup pales in comparison to learning the skill needed for a real hunt.

Yet you say legal hunting season is just a snatch of time—the rest of the year stretches out to ad infinitum. I agree, but you can duplicate a hunt any time you provide the birds. And you do this either by patronizing a landowner who has them on his property or supplying your own in several ways discussed up front.

My point is this, and I cannot emphasize it enough, if you've got two hours to spend with Pup, don't stand there throwing those damnable dummies or running inconsequential drills. Get him into birds. Then more birds. And if you live in a state stupid enough to outlaw training on wild birds, then move. For a state that out of it will probably pass even worse legislation to ruin your life.

If you tire of toting birds to field and gathering them up and working with counterfeit feather, then take Pup to a game preserve and shoot those birds. Game preserves are taking over the land. There's one close to you. They ain't bona fide hunting, but it ain't you and Pup laying on the couch, either.

And, of course, you find that place where wild birds abound. And you present the best of yourself you ever were, and the kind man who owns the land where the birds abound says, "Sure, you can train on them." Now you've got it. Real birds for wild bird training for the wild bird hunt.

Think of it. There's nothing else that matters, that is as productive, as exciting, as motivating for Pup. Real birds. Wild birds. Bird training. For the hunt.

And don't shy away from buying, keeping, and handling birds because you've never done it before. Talk to your supplier. He'll be glad to tell you what to do, what to avoid. And if you have a calamity and lose your birds, then get in touch with the agricultural extension agent in your area or your local land-bank college, and they'll tell you exactly what went wrong.

Game biologists working for your fish and game commission are also there to help you, to bring you along, to make sure you get it right. Use them.

But don't ever let me catch you standing in the street with Pup at side, yelling, "Heel, sit, stay!" That's the wrong drill, in the wrong place, as are most drills outlined by obsolete training books.

Just remember, if it has nothing to do with birds, it has nothing to do with you and Pup. Matter of fact, that statement is so important, go to a sign painter and have him letter that on both front doors of your new four-wheel-drive pickup with the custom kennel bed. Memorize just that one sentence, and you'll have gotten your money's worth from this book. I repeat:

If it has nothing to do with birds, it has nothing to do with you and Pup.

Now a final word about bonding and imprinting.

*If it has nothing to do with birds, it has nothing to do with you and Pup. (Photograph ©
Larry Anderson)*

The Bonded,
or Imprinted, Dog

*"I no longer train my dogs. I imprint with them
and they train themselves. You do the same and yours will too."*
—Author

Webster's *New World Dictionary:*
BOND: A binding or uniting force; tie; link. Anything that binds, fastens, or restrains.

IMPRINTING: A learning mechanism operating very early in the life of an animal, in which a particular stimulus immediately establishes an irreversible behavior pattern with reference to the same stimulus in the future.

And that stimulus is you.

ADOPTING AN INFANT PUP
Absolute Warning: If you can't give thirty days to the infant pup—four to five weeks old at adoption—then there's no way you can imprint. You may bond but not imprint. Also there is this: To every rule there is the exception. Jim Culbertson's little black bitch, Keg of Black Powder, was the greatest Labrador retriever I ever saw or ever will see.

Yet, she was rejected as a pup; lived nine months without stimulus in her home kennel; was then adopted by Jim, who had never trained a Lab in his life; and she became the greatest hunter I ever popped a cap over and won both her open and amateur field trial championships.

Imprint when Pup first comes home, then bond. (Photograph © Gary Kramer)

So go with what I say but know that there's nothing ironclad under the sun.

The pup that imprints has got to be in a kennel crate at eye level when you're sleeping in bed. It is you who must awaken, however, as many times a night that is required to take him or her outdoors to tinkle. The pup has to be at your feet when you eat, at your side when reading the newspaper or watching TV, beside you in your vehicle when you run an errand.

He must be taken to field where he can run and snoop, you must maintain a supply of various game birds at all time. The pup must have complete access to your house and home; he must be able to look up or sniff around and find you at all times.

He must have unlimited play time with you—in the play is his future work.

Then and only then will you imprint.

Therefore, you cannot attempt to approach this halfway or part-time and accomplish a gun dog that is your duplicate in psyche, mind, body, and soul. When you walk, the pup walks. When you sigh, the pup sighs. He is you. Your clone. Your Siamese twin.

This is the dog that when you decide the birds are in the hedge row to the left—he will cast left.

When you think there's ducks on the pond and drop to your knees, sneaking forward—he will sneak forward, too.

With no discussion, no prompting.

For he is you. One heart, one mind, one purpose.

And he reads your mind, near or afar. He knows what you're thinking sometimes before you do. He becomes mystical and beyond comprehension.

Like Jim Pettijohn's Labrador Booze. Jim was a pilot for TWA. In the beginning of his career he bid for flights and got the leavings, so his wife, Gloria, never knew where Jim had flown or when he was coming home. But up to two days before even Jim knew his schedule, Booze would take his place at the door of their home. Booze knew.

That's the gun dog I want for you.

I have been blessed with imprinted dogs the past twenty years. They are a humbling experience and they are a great obligation, for they have given their life to you, and you must care for that life and respect that life.

They cannot think any other way than you do, so you think only in

You'll be amazed what a little act of kindness will accomplish; don't let Pup down. (Photograph © Lon E. Lauber)

ways to please them, to help them, to cherish them.

No way could you shock, shoot, kick, strike, or in any way punish this dog. He is helpless, for everything he is has been handed over to you. He is defenseless.

But then it would never come to pass you'd have to correct this dog, for he is so interpretive of your mind, he can only do what you're thinking.

Therefore this is the new age of gun dog training, the ultimate result. Those who still resort to dominance, pain, and exasperation are to be pitied, but not so much as their dogs, for their dogs are the helpless victims.

BONDING

Now you can bond, and that's great, too. Not as ironclad as imprinting, but still better than just training a dog the old-fashioned way and then taking him hunting.

You can bond with a dog adopted at seven weeks. You can bond with a dog with only part of your time spent in imprinting.

Keith Strawder, Kansas City, Missouri, admires a brace of gadwalls while his Lab, Sky, raises a tentative leg as if to ask, "Did I do alright, Boss?" (Photograph © Larry Anderson)

And this is probably the reality for you.

For you do not work at home, so you don't have all this time to "be" with Pup. And you're not there for all the little special things, like eating lunch, then telling Pup to jump in the truck and driving him around the block.

Or stopping at the Dairy Queen and buying him an ice cream cone. You'll be amazed at what a little act of kindness will accomplish.

I remember fifteen years ago when Terry Smith of Decaturville, Tennessee, and I were going duck hunting and we stopped at a McDonald's and bought each dog a Big Mac. It was only one bite apiece, but you should have seen the joy in their eyes. And it's always a joy that's paid back. Those Labs did glomp the mud on that hunt.

Except for your spouse, that dog is the best friend you've got. Don't let him down. Always think of a kindness to give him. For that's exactly the way he thinks regarding you.

And remember: with any dog the miracle of an imprinted pup nears the realm of magic. The wand we use to touch the star and make it dazzle is YOU.

Epilogue

I wrote this book on the eve of the twenty-first century, a century that will see public consensus and statutory law bring to pass everything we seek in this book.

Our past age of promoting dominance over dogs, the sanctioning of brutality in training, and our archaic past of considering a dog's worth as nothing more than chattel will finally end.

All torture instruments presently used on a dog in the name of training will be outlawed, and humans will be astounded with the joy of bonding with a love-trained dog, who'll attain levels of performance impossible to achieve with force methods.

I'm sorry I'll not be present to see all I speak of here, but I am happy to have been a part of bringing it to reality. And I want you to know I'm indebted to each of you for going forward, for putting rivets into this dream.

And the scream of some dog's desperation at the hands of an idiot will be heard no more.

(Photograph © Kent and Donna Dannen)

Index

About the Author

The late Bill Tarrant is nationally recognized as the pioneer in humane gun dog training. He based his beliefs not only on morality but also on results. Bill unequivocally declared "domination in gun dog training is dead" and added that if a trainer bonds with his dog, "a look of disappointment on the trainer's face hurts an errant dog more than if he had been beat down by a 2 x 4."

For more than a quarter century, Bill served as gun dog editor for *Field & Stream*, writing some 350 articles for the magazine up until his death. He authored thirteen books on dogs, including *Gun Dog Training: New Strategies from Today's Top Trainers* and *Hey Pup, Fetch It Up!: The Complete Retriever Training Book*. He was named Writer of the Year by the Outdoor Writers Association of America, the Purina corporation, and the Dog Writers Association of America, the latter honoring him with the award twice. He also received the Orvis Award for Distinguished Outdoor Literature. Bill died in 1998.